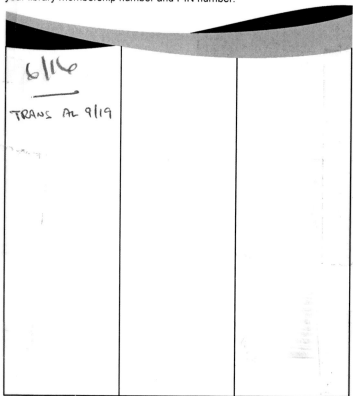

# mpT
## MODERN POETRY
## IN TRANSLATION

*The best of world poetry*

No.1 2016
© *Modern Poetry in Translation* 2016 and contributors

ISSN (print) 0969-3572
ISSN (online) 2052-3017
ISBN (print) 978-1-91048-509-5
ISBN (ebook) 978-1-91048-510-1

Editor: Sasha Dugdale
Managing Editor: Deborah de Kock
Web and Communications Manager: Ed Cottrell
Design by Katy Mawhood
Cover art by Molly Crabapple

Printed and bound in Great Britain by Charlesworth Press, Wakefield
For submissions and subscriptions please visit www.mptmagazine.com

Modern Poetry in Translation Limited. A Company Limited by Guarantee
Registered in England and Wales, Number 5881603
UK Registered Charity Number 1118223

 Supported using public funding by
## ARTS COUNCIL
## ENGLAND

Modern Poetry in Translation gratefully acknowledges the support of the British
Council and is proud to be part of Refugee Week.

 BRITISH COUNCIL

 Refugee Week

# MODERN POETRY IN TRANSLATION

## *The Great Flight*

# CONTENTS

## Focus

## Essays & Reviews

# EDITORIAL

Molly Crabapple, the cover artist for this special refugee issue of MPT, sent me a portrait in response to the poems I sent her from the issue. When I asked Molly to write about the subject of the portrait she replied:

This is a portrait of my friend Zoza, a Kurdish artist from Aleppo. An early supporter of the revolution, Zoza finally had to leave Syria in 2014, and now, like so many Syrians in exile, lives in Gaziantep, Turkey. We met working on a mural at a school for Syrian refugee kids in the border town of Reyhanli. Zoza paints like Francis Bacon sometimes, but his day job is working as a graphic designer for an NGO supporting refugees.

The striking thing about Hozan Kaya Jan (Zoza), in Molly's sketch, is his realness. There is no possibility that this man, with his electric-blue-inked curls and his thoughtful, slightly sardonic gaze, is a figment of anyone's artistic or journalistic imagination. He looks out and challenges us to reduce him to an infographic or a statistic. He stands in iconic opposition to the ugly notions of refugees swarming into Europe like rats or cockroaches, or even the apparently more positive notion of pitiful hordes of victims. Zoza is a separate and complex existence, as we all are: complex, ineffable creatures, caught somewhere on this planet and dealing with it as best we can.

Molly responded to the poems in this way, because the poems are also irreducible. The voices in this focus issue are so blastingly individual, that even the noise of flight and migration recedes when you read, for example, Nasrin Parvaz's anger at the discrimination inherent in not offering asylum seekers the opportunity to learn

**HOZAN KAYA JAN:** 'OK this painting started a long time ago when i first left Aleppo and came to Turkey. It's keeping together from the first day all the personalities i have all the faces i live on daily basis, all the memories i don't wanna let go, all former life i had i never wanna forget. [...] It's the bodiless form, i don't know if it's a correct word, i feel i am having... big dreams yet no legs to go forward.'

English, or Amarjit Chandan's chance meeting with a Punjabi compatriot in the Barcelona metro. What general point can be drawn from this focus, except that politics and war have the power to make us all homeless, wandering, and dependent on the kindness of strangers? We'd better hope that when it happens we meet with more compassion than many refugees have had from us.

I was anxious that publishing poems seemed an empty gesture. After all, I reasoned, what current refugees need right now is not poems, but aid: warmth, food and medical help. But the response of the Assyrian poets published in the issue, many of whom are living in refugee camps, persuaded me that publishing this work as part of a focus on refugees was the right thing to do. The President of the Syriac Writers Union said that it had 'turned their sadness into happiness' to know their poems had reached the UK. It mattered to them that their voices had not been extinguished as their ordinary lives had.

And what can we do, except to continue to believe in our own form of the Republic of Letters: MPT as a virtual and metaphysical utopia where poets of all races and places meet and share poetry? It's a minute and fragile vision, and the tiniest drop of cynicism pollutes it in seconds like a pipette of radioactive material. Yet it lasts: fifty years after it was founded at a point of cataclysm in Europe, it continues quietly publishing its republic of poets in the face of war and cataclysm around the world.

*Sasha Dugdale*

MPT is donating all the royalties from its fiftieth anniversary anthology *Centres of Cataclysm* published by Bloodaxe Books to the Refugee Council. More details at www.bloodaxebooks.com

# GËZIM HAJDARI

Translated by Viktor Berberi

Gëzim Hajdari's many poetic works range from the sparse, at times lapidary, lyric, to the dramatic monologue (*Maldiluna*, 'Moonsick'), to the epic (*Nur: Besa ed eresia*, 'Nur: Oath and Heresy'), to contemporary translations of traditional oral forms (*I canti dei nizàm*, 'Songs of the Nizam') and the expansive poem-denunciation (*Poema dell'esilio*, 'Poem of Exile'). The arc of Hajdari's career demonstrates the courage with which he has held tight to his own voice, however at odds with contemporary trends in Italian literature. Perhaps the most striking aspect of Hajdari's work is its complete dedication to renewing poetry's task of speaking as the voice of its time. As he tends the memory of a people's past, Hajdari documents the existential condition of the exile and migrant and calls his readers to an encounter with other worlds.

An outspoken critic of both the Communist and post-Communist political class in Albania, Hajdari has collected accounts of the innumerable literary figures persecuted under Hoxha's regime in his *Gjëmë: Genocidi i poezisë shqipe* (Funeral Lament: The Genocide of Albanian Poetry). Indeed, his entire output can be read as a struggle to restore a voice to the voiceless, whether those suppressed by a brutal dictatorship, those who have been forced to abandon their homelands, or the others left behind to suffer poverty and violence. The following poems are characterized by a movement across borders (cultural, political, linguistic) and between present and past, looking back from Hajdari's current home in Italy to the landscape, language and legends of the Albanian province of Darsìa. Hajdari's great gift to Italian literature lies in his having brought to bear in his contemporary poems in Italian the richness of an ancient Balkan, and, more specifically, northern Albanian, epic tradition.

## Perhaps in the Naked Hills of Darsìa...

Perhaps in the naked hills of Darsìa
my fragile verses will be buried
under the dry thorns of the pomegranate tree
struck by the icy winds of the East.

Far from the young girls' loves
that will never know their anguish,
solitary under the black sky
like the robin in the darkness of winter.

The rustling of the grass, the blackbird's song
will accompany their lament.
While autumn's brief nights
will cover them with a pale moon.

## The Ones Who Continue to Flee in the Snow...

The ones who continue to flee in the snow,
leaving behind them shrunken skies,
fragile, trembling walls,
are at the mercy of an unknown home
and the night's pale moon.

Why are they driven to obliterate memories
and give up their nostalgia?

And the ashes of the dead, the altars,
what will they come to?

Turn toward recollection, bless
the trampled flowers, the water of the wells
from which you have drunk,
they will protect you through the exile you have undertaken:
among enchanted woods
and pitiless seasons.

## You Exist in the Face of Winter...

You exist in the face of winter
as a wound. Motionless and foreign
in an imperfect space, never welcoming,
waiting for the sand's even silence
to speak to you in secret.
Don't be astonished by the wandering river and new trees
that were not here before. All around the transience
of things, the disappearance of poets who bind
heaven to land, will continue.
It is said we will die in opposing lands.
My years: an escape into the unknown
and waking again frightened in the night.

## I Fall Back into the Nothingness...

I fall back into the nothingness
and keep my secrets hidden.

On the hills
the wind moves

the white sheets
of the dead.

Anonymous faces are silent
because they are unable to cry.

To whom does one turn
in this sterile land?

Like a sorrowful monk
I bury in the dark soil
flowers fallen from the almond tree.

## Every Day I Create a New Homeland...

Every day I create a new homeland
in which I die and am reborn,
a nation without maps or flags,
celebrated by your deep eyes
that follow me always
on the voyage toward fragile heavens.
In all lands I sleep, enamoured,
in any home I wake a child,
my key can open any border
and the doors of any black prison.
My being is eternal return and departure
from one fire to the next, from water to water.
The anthem of my nations: the blackbird's song
that I sing in seasons of setting moons,
moons that have risen from your brow of darkness and stars
with the eternal will of the sun-god.

## How Poor We Are...

How poor we are.
I live from one day to the next in Italy,
you, in our homeland, can't even drink a coffee.

Our fault: we love,
our sentence: to live alone, divided
by dark water.

I will come back in the fall like Constantine,
in our native hills you have already gathered the oregano
I will take with me into my empty room.

Now I live in place of myself
far from that land that without pity
devours its children.

NOTE: In the poem 'How Poor We Are...' Constantine, or the Knight of Death, is a character from the most beautiful of the oral tales of the Arbëresh, the ethnic Albanian communities of southern Italy. These tales have as their principal motif the *besa*, the traditional Albanian word of honour.

# BASUKI GUNAWAN

Translated by David Colmer

Basuki Gunawan (1929–2014) was an Indonesian who travelled to
the Netherlands as a student in the early fifties and ended up staying
and becoming a respected sociologist. As a family friend I was asked
to read the English translation of a poem that he had written at his
funeral in 2014: 'I Fill the Earth With My Song'. There had never
been a Dutch version and the original Indonesian was thought lost,
but looking at the English, and the German translation it had been
based on, I was struck by the power of the poem. There were a few
points where I wondered if the right translation choices had been
made and this led me to do a search which, immediately and to my
surprise, yielded an Indonesian site with the original versions of this
and twelve other poems as well as five short stories, all published in
the mid-fifties.

The site was dedicated in part to 'forgotten' Indonesian writers
and maintained by Veronica B. Vonny, who in 1997 had written
her thesis on Gunawan's work, arguing that he had been unfairly
neglected and had actually played a leading role in introducing
existentialism, surrealism and nonconventional narrative forms
into Indonesian fiction. She, in turn, besides being saddened to
have missed the opportunity to contact her literary hero herself, was
amazed to discover that he had lived such a long life and fascinated
to hear that he had also written an excellent novella in Dutch.

An appraisal of the Indonesian originals of the poems showed
that the 1950s German translation had been quite free and the 1960s
English translation had drifted even further away from the originals
as a result. These new translations give precedence to the original
Indonesian.

The translator thanks Heri Lesmana Hardjo and Indrawati
Gunawan for their help and advice, and acknowledges the German

translations of W. A. Braasem and Janheinz Jahn, published in *Reis und Hahnenschrei*, an anthology of Indonesian poetry, (1957) and Ulli Beier's translations from the German, published in the chapbook *Only Dust* (1969).

## *I Fill the Earth With My Song...*

I fill the earth with my song
I stab mankind with my plea
for alms
a cup of hope
a bowl of love
because the land
where the sun's lament is over
and the cock has stopped its crowing
is not far
the street is lonely
as a cemetery
but far from it
because this dying
is a guttersnipe
who taunts the passers-by
I fill the earth with my song
I stab mankind with my plea.

## I Once Knew a God...

I once knew a god
we played together
drinking cordial eating cake
now god is gone
did he run away?
I saw him in the treetops
a mist descended in search of god
then carried him up
to the stars
god is happy there
drinking cordial eating cake
but here the trees shed tears of blood
and curses rain from the sun
a thousand gods howl in the sky.


## Beloved

Yes I know
you are a bottomless sea
a place where silvery fish
satisfy their hunger with time and space
until only shells are scattered about.

## Night Butterfly

Your lips are soft and moist
like a doormat trodden
by a thousand joyous feet
rushing into the chamber of lust
whose walls are smothered with dust
only dust.

## It's Time...

It's time
the moon is nodding off
in its blue chair
let's go
don't look back
jackals are already devouring our tracks
filling the sky with footsteps and dust
making virgins tremble in lonely beds
awakening gales
hurry
before heaven closes its gate
before we shrivel to ash.

# LUCRETIUS

Translated by Emma Gee

We know almost nothing about Lucretius, except a story, probably made up centuries after his life, that he drank a love potion, went mad and died before putting the final gloss on his work, his *De rerum natura*, 'On the Nature of the Universe', written c.55 BC. It is a poem, in six books of Latin hexameters, which explains every aspect of the world through two components only: atoms and void. Its physical system encompasses everything, from the quantum to the very large; from the identity of the human self to the physics of colour.

Lucretius' work is not abstruse or irrelevant. Its immediacy is breathtaking: science is an urgent task; religion can and should be critiqued with glorious abandon; we must rethink the lies and delusions we shore our lives up with. He speaks to us as much as to his Roman audience – challenges us, makes us hoot with laughter, provokes indignation, shame, anxiety. This is not so much because we see the embryo of our own contemporary thought in him, although this is also true; but because we still *feel*.

Lucretius' text was transmitted to the modern age by the slenderest of threads. The text disappeared between antiquity and the Middle Ages, until its rediscovery in 1417. There's little doubt that, though the historical and physical connection between us and Lucretius is so exiguous, his impact on Western culture is one of nuclear ferocity.

This is not a translation, although I have consulted Lucretius for every word and agonized over every hexameter, with an awareness of the issues Classical scholarship brings to the text. Where there is metaphor in the text I have often replaced it with my own, contemporary image; where there's visual wordplay with letters, or soundplay with phonemes, as there frequently is, I have aspired to equivalence in visual texture or sonority, not necessarily

in translation. I have retained Lucretius' 'formulaic' repetitions,
but not slavishly. I have resisted the urge of English to dissolve into
iambic pentameters, and tried to convey the roughness of Lucretius'
sound-world.

## *Atoms Are Eternal*

atoms live forever
though their colours are expressed in different weaves
things don't unravel
until they meet with that degree of tearing
balanced to their weft.

even then they don't degrade to nil –
everything just resolves
into its Primary Parts.

the raindrops Father Sky scatters
in the womb of Mother Earth –
these seem to die
but then we see
the shining spikes of crops
prick though the land;
the neon green of foliage
lights up the branches
the trees stoop down to give us fruit –
us and the beasts.

from this source we see cities
put forth their flowers of children

from here the woods' uncurling fronds
sing all about with voices of new birds;

herds make a lying-place in crushed grass
tired of schlepping their fat about
and leave a stamp of themselves
upon the richness of their fodder
their tight udders a snowy freefall of milk drops

from this source too their newborn calves
lurch across green velvet fields
on crazy limbs, trying to play,
high on milk too pure for their tiny minds.

of everything we see
nothing perishes foundation-up:
it's all about exchange of matter
nothing dies that doesn't gift a life.

## Venus

Imagine there's a god
a goddess even
let's call her the Goddess of Love
no Botticelli Venus climbing out of a shell
but Nature – anarchic Aphrodite;
she builds things up then kicks them
down again like an angry toddler.

the selfish gene, the pleasure principle
she fills to brim the ship-enduring sea
crop-heavy earth; coaxes every living thing
beneath the sliding signs of heaven
to leap into the light.

the clouds scud escort when she comes
Architect Earth throws down the red carpet
the mirror sea blinks back the smiling sky.

she flings the veil from day's Spring face
shoots down the little birds midair
each one a sounding bell
struck through the heart
the whole dawn chorus a reckless
cascade of notes tumbling
mi-re-do
down from above.

bent on increase she
goads every species wild or tame
to buck the winter off
cross seas and mountains
ford foamy rivers
follow where libido leads
in an orgy of replication.

you too: she'll flatter you
into thinking you're in love; seduce you
with cottonwool clouds and lambs
lull you with soft summer –

then she'll say: 'Think you can come at me
with your dragnets and carbon footprint?
I'll truss your machismo up
and crack your neck till you beg for mercy.'

can this dominatrix turn
our wars to love? of course, for she rules all:
without her no sun would ever rise
above the holy borderlands of light.

she's the god I'd call
to beat my song's bronze gong:
the tart who starts the music,
turns the stars, turns you on.

## Time

Time has no existence of its own
outside our need for order:
what's done in time past
what begs our attention now
which result will follow.
time is a human fabrication:
it has no abstract life
apart from things in rest and things in motion.

history's an illusion
an accident of nature
whether on a global or a village scale:
world wars, genocide

the Scandals of the Old House –
be careful these don't take on
the lives of characters
in an historical drama
living in the here-and-now:
these events were products
of specific times, specific races
now (thank god) consigned to
death's oblivion.

History is a Trojan Horse of the mind:
it infiltrates walled cities
and fans the flames of war
by stealthy parturition of ideas.

we allow ourselves to be seduced
by history's illusion like a love-story:
it's kindled in our hearts no less
than a lover's face in an adulterer's breast.

we like to think there's more to life
than bodies moving about in space:
but in reality
there is no possible reconstruction
of any momentary union of Void and Body
events we can base ideas on
such as justice, love or peace:

just the chance coalescence of the past.

## Wind

Think about phenomena whose only explanation
is the behaviour of unseen particles.
first among these is wind.
wind's whirling lashes white horses
swoops on ships
rips clouds like kids pull fairy floss apart

other times
it builds up to a rant from threatening mutter
courses plains, a lethal spinning cone
or winds about the woods
and when it leaves
the hills are dressed in matchstick tresses
like Mount St Helens
just by force of air.

wind's matter, dark to sight
sweeps like a massive broom
the sea, sweeps earth, sweeps
the clouds of heaven even,
snatching them in sudden eddy -

wind is like a river
only one you can't see.

its unseen forces
proliferate destruction by impulse
just as when water's gentle nature
suddenly turns nasty

when rain upstream
brings about a personality shift
a mountain-fed apocalypse
measuring its water pressure in tens of tons
grabs whole chunks of forest, little islands
with mini plantations riding on them
grinds boulders in its way
like ball bearings
then hurls them down
a lethal Niagara
brushes ancient bridges aside
with a dismissive gesture
and spreads destruction's effluent everywhere.

gusts of wind have to behave the same:
with the same muscle as a river
they fall upon locations at their whim
propel things before their breath's rocket thrust
snatch them up when impulse takes them
in a great spinning cone which walks the earth
poised in gravity-defying slow motion
while at its core a hungry vortex
whirls too fast for the eye to see.

with equal force
my reiterated hammer-blows of proof
break open wind's matter dark to sight
and so we see it engaged in underhanded emulation
of acts which in rivers are overt.

# CAITLÍN MAUDE

Translated by Doireann Ní Ghríofa

Some time ago, I was invited to give a lecture on Irish language poetry at the Irish Writers' Centre. As I read, one poem in particular took me by surprise – 'Aimhréidh' by Caitlín Maude. It's a poem that I've loved for years, but I had always read it silently, alone. I looked out to the audience and noticed that some people were weeping. Maude's poetry assumes a greater poignancy due to what we know of the poet's life – that she died of cancer at the age of just 41, leaving bereft a husband, a young son, family and friends, and many admirers of her work.

Caitlín Maude was a writer who loved Dublin, and felt creatively nourished by all the rush and noise of the city. That night, as I walked past pubs, taxis and chippers, I felt her walk with me. I had been awarded a residency at the Tyrone Guthrie Centre and just before I left, I was told by a friend of Maude's that she, too, had visited in the last year of her life. I spent many mornings reading and translating Caitlín's poems to English, and thought of her often as I sat at my desk and gazed out at Annamaghkerrig Lake. She, too, must have looked at that glassy surface during her stay.

A versatile artist, aside from her work in literature, theatre, and politics, Caitlín Maude is perhaps best known for her music. She was a gifted singer in the traditional sean-nós style, and in recordings, her voice lilts high as a lark. We are fortunate to be left with the legacy of Caitlín's poems, this beautiful echo of her life. Across the decades, her words sing to us, still.

My gratitude to Caomhán Ó Luain, Caitlín's son, who gave permission last year for these translations to be published.

## Driving the Cattle

It is neither watercress
nor food
bitter undertooth
this cud
which I chew fiercely
this fitting taste of my days
'hup! Ya bitch, hup!
if it was the right gap
you wanted to avoid
on you go then my dear, onwards,
a day of long grass stretches kindly for you
I chew keenly
of my bitter cud
until I empty
I chew until
the lustrous saliva fills
to teeth
and the spittle
I cast out fiercely.

A ripe bulk
of berries sweetens
along the path.

# Captivity

I am an animal

a wild animal
from the tropics
celebrated far and wide
for my beauty

once
I'd shake the forest trees
with my roar

but now
I lie down
and stare through one eye
at that solitary tree over there

people come in their hundreds
every day

who would do anything at all
for me
except release me.

## Poem

We live from day to day
with 'more' and 'less'
death and life

it is not a petty smell
    the smell of death
but the smell of life
    is an immense smell

it's a small constriction
the constriction of death
but too great a catch in the throat
is the deep emotion of life

## A Spell of Work

Hand me a hammer
or a hatchet
that I might smash
and batter
this house
that I might make a threshold
of the lintel
and floors of the walls
that all the sod-scraw
and roof and
chimney would come down
with the strength of my sweat

Now, hand me over
the boards and the nails
till I build
this other houss...

But oh Lord, I am tired!

# SAKYIL TSETA

Translated by Tenzin Dickyi

Sakyil Tseta is a poet and essayist, from the town of Rebkong in north-eastern Tibet and a member of the Third Generation, a new group of Tibetan poets and writers constituting a new literary movement centered around the border town of Xiling (Xining in Qinghai) at the edge of the Tibetan plateau. These writers write primarily in Tibetan as opposed to Chinese. Sakyil published his first piece in a literary magazine run by the local monastery, and since then he has published his work in all four of the Third Generation anthologies of contemporary Tibetan writing. 'Rebkong' was published in March 2013 on the popular and prestigious online journal *Gedun Chopel*. The poem is an ode to the poet's hometown Rebkong, which has a hallowed place in the Tibetan consciousness – it has produced many of Tibet's most famous scholars and writers and is known for being a literary and intellectual cradle. This poem is a celebration and assertion of, and also mourning for, Tibetan identity, culture and history.

## *Rebkong*

Burn the offering of incense, blow the dharma conch.
You are a blue altar for incense,
You are a dark fairy tale from long ago.

O Rebkong, black fort of history
Where my father's bones decayed,
My mother's vital spirit scattered.

Sometimes you are like the cool breeze

Streaming through the high mountains,
Sometimes like the clear water
Sluicing through the low valley.
Precious to the king's heart like its heartblood boiling,
Is the glittering Rongwo monastery
A black tent resplendent amid blue grass?
Or a line of young wild yaks on mountain crags?

O Rebkong, fatherland.
Famed Rebkong of history where the dust has not yet settled.
You are a song to sing, a dance to dance,
Where the poor dream joyful dreams,
The rich display coloured turquoise and corals
And the lonely down their drinks in one shot.

Every morning and every evening,
The red valley is wreathed in a belt of smoke,
Like the chest of a freshly slain yak,
As the smoke rises, curling into air.

Where there is cause and effect,
Whatever the season or the time of day,
When I bind my pain and gaze at it,
You leap at times into the sky, an eagle,
At times fall into the water like an autumn leaf.

This may be the sinful
Karma of your unhappy deed,
The divining sign
That your soul-stone will disintegrate.

No matter, O Rebkong,
From the clean drizzle of spring rain,
The soft fragile shoots of green grass –
This leaf, like your smile:
This leaf is your love.

Rebkong, you cannot be
The string-less dragon-headed *piwang*,
You cannot be the round moon with no shade.

No matter who catches cold,
You give the first sneeze.
No matter in whose kitchen there's a fire,
You are where the smoke rises.

Rebkong, is it the Guchu river that falls as your teardrops,
The heart of your history cut open?
Now the Guchu knows no waves or billows, no pristine transparence.

At the source of the Guchu, a self-deceiving
Mirror bobs in the water,
A mirror to piece the locals' hearts,
Bobbing, gently bobbing.

O Rebkong, you who are a Great Mother to me.
When the rocking mirror no longer reflects me,
Your artistry, your intelligence, your ancestors –
Who will care for them? Who will fly
The windhorses to bring us fortune?

O Rebkong, spring fled long ago
From the teeth of months and years,
Why are you deep still in winter's sleep?

Do the villagers, done breaking up
The new year's fried *khabseys*,
Now prepare, without doubting
The weather, to pick caterpillar fungus
At the base of Jhakyung Mountain?
Is it the caterpillar fungus that gives you
Energy for body and spirit
Neglecting neither soul nor marrow?

Even if Grandmother's stories ignite a butter lamp in you,
Even if Grandfather's plough animals give you confidence,
Even so, you are not the skinless dark rocky mountain,
Nor the giant who shores up the glory of the sun and the moon.


**NOTE:** *Piwang* is the two-stringed Tibetan fiddle; *Khabsey* are
fried homemade biscuits.

# NGARMA

Translated by Tenzin Dickyi

Ngarma is a young and emerging poet,from Amdo in north-eastern Tibet. The poem was published in *Gedun Chopel* in 2011. Ngarma also wrote the lyrics for the song 'New Generation' by the Tibetan rock band Yudrug, which has become an anthem for Tibetan youth in both Tibet and in the exile diaspora around the world. Ngarma is the pen name of the poet Jigshel Kyab. Tibetan writers often use only pen names and the word *Ngarma* means 'the angry one'.

## An Old Man's Present

Only twenty three and a mountain range of regret.
What is this? What is this?

From the door I invite a drop of light.
Dust particles
Assemble here.

The tea has long grown cold.
Much that has cooled cannot be warmed again.

All these various incomplete drawings can't be erased.
I can't forget unfinished works.
Breaking the three unbroken arrows on my clock,
I disarranged the twelve numbered hours,
In the morning, hid from myself wrinkles on my forehead.

A vehicle drags a tail of black smoke,
Rushes east at dawn and returns west at night.

Near the highway
I see a couple kissing happily,
I see in my mind
Not my past but their future.

Only dreams plumb the mind's depths.
The forgetful mind
Makes me feather light.

One day, as you see me flying –
That's an illusion,
But another carrying me –
That's real.

My hair fell and grew.
My eyes popped out of the dark.

As the thorn-bird loves the thorn,
So I love the world.

My steps grow smaller,
My body bends.
One by one I forget names
Inked in the letter sleeping in this desk
Facing me.

Those brought away by guardians of the dead must be dead,
I have received no response from my friends.

In another place, at another time,
In a smoke-filled bar, they ponder
Country and neighbour, regret
My late arrival.

The darkness is like closely-laid black bricks.
I recognize everywhere as my home.
And in my home, there is no fire even in winter,
No flowers even in summer.

Various objects in the distance
Burn in the distance.
Images I can see have their essence,
So do my birth, growth, sickness and death,
An essence that is interlinked.

How do they connect,
Smells and sounds that can't be touched,
That collapse and scatter,
And the root of my soul scattering?
How do they connect, my soul
And clouds that glide overhead?

The owl swooping in the armpit of night
Lands on wingtips of white light.
This town is the inner heart of chaos.

I have spent my days and nights
On its streets and shops and bookstores.
With an old key from my front pocket,
I open an old door, lay on an old bed

Dreaming old dreams. The news is today's
But I feel like yesterday.

Right now even an hour is a single rosary bead refusing to move,
Rolling my thumb is all the duty I can manage.

Just now there can be an afterlife.
Or there can be no afterlife.

# PIERLUIGI CAPPELLO

Translated by Todd Portnowitz

Though born in Gemona del Friuli, Pierluigi Cappello's memories
are often set in the nearby city of Chiusaforte – a city of no more
than 800 inhabitants in a valley of the Alps, all but cut off from
the cultural and political fluctuations of the Italian peninsula. Just
north are the borders of Austria and Slovenia. To the southeast is
Trieste, once home to the poet Umberto Saba, with whom Cappello
shares a troubled, lyrical simplicity and a deep allegiance to his
surrounding landscape. As ardently as Italy has claimed him as its
poet, awarding him the Viareggio Répaci prize for his 2010 collection
*Mandate a dire all'imperatore* (Go Tell It to the Emperor), as well as
the Bagutta Opera Prima prize and the Montale Europa prize for
previous collections, Cappello remains distinctly Friulian, with two
volumes of poetry published in his region's dialect.

In 1976 a 6.5 magnitude earthquake tore Friuli apart, killing
nearly 1,000 and leaving over 150,000 without a home. Cappello and
his family were transferred to a prefab community provided as relief
by the Austrians, where he's lived nearly all of his adult life, confined
by his limited mobility after a near-fatal motorbike accident at
the age of sixteen. Like end words in a sestina, the things of Friuli
loop in and out of his poems: snow, fir trees, swallows, stones. And
people. For Cappello, to summon in memory is to give life. He calls
upon the figures of his past not merely to evoke a mood or an image
for the reader, but for his own pleasure, to relish their company.

In his craft, Cappello is a patient, subtle magician, reminiscent
of late Merwin in *The Shadow of Sirius*. With sleight of hand he shifts
a word, pulls a comma, swaps verb for noun, and so transports the
reader to a realm of meaning not above language but behind it – the
alphabet pulled back like a curtain to reveal a bare stage, haunting
and dream-abiding. In the translations below I have attempted

to mirror his special syntax and sparse punctuation wherever possible, to recreate for the reader in English the same enchanting disorientation I felt upon approaching these poems for the first time in Italian.

## *April, Playground*

In April, as a child,
the trees wore mitres,
raised their heads in long
long liturgies,
and a luminous silence opened
a temple in the clouds;
today
a long ago mid-April
throughout this silence
not one hides its head in its hands
seated, I place my temples in a clearing of sky –
they should be loved,
all of them, every one by someone;
instead each shakes its greyness out
and shadows go by living
in celebration as if they'd lived
orphan of all that moves
spring is in the sight of its reflection
on the thin hair of your forearms in the sun.

## Summer Poem

Still here, still how
still ever
as where we are
when it begins
the green begins
where the string-course ends
a breeze runs through
cool hedges in the shade
their shapely stillness
the gaze trailing off;
I smoke my morning cigarette
to remind you of dawn:
a blonde, capillary flash
like a birth, and it's gone;
a billow of breasts
in a white silk blouse
you wave as you approach
the Sunday of my eyes
the clean contentedness of seeing
things in the persistence of things.
It's a reminder
that it leaves you every day.

## Evening

Nine o'clock, evening, and a bit of the black that stains your hands
the earth entire has rolled through here
what time do the bees drift off, you think, you wonder
you press the hollow of your hand to the edge of your knee;
and in telling yourself you feel how new the leaves are
from which particular loneliness they've flown
you take things now as they come
and plant themselves before you, when within you
and ever so slightly you let your head nod into absence,
into the question of what hour the bees drift off
when the savour of earth and the clouds
passed before my years, together.

# LOUISE LABÉ

Translated by Olivia McCannon

Who could resist the sonnets of Louise Labé? The tone of voice is immediately compelling, weighing face-to-face directness with fully rounded wit. These are poems which speak to everyone – candidly assertive, warmly human – as if five hundred years were nothing.

Louise Labé's life – like the lives of so many women of talent – has frequently received more attention than her work. It has been shaped into a scandal (she was a courtesan), a legend (she rode to war), and most recently, a sham (she was a man). But perhaps she was just born in the right place at the right time: to an enlightened father who gave her access to the same education (fencing, riding, poetry, other languages) as her brothers; in Lyon, thriving cultural crossroads of the Renaissance.

The importance and pleasure of the work, notably the 24 Petrarchan sonnets she published alongside her *Débat de folie et d'amour*, in 1555, seem indisputable, at least. Labé's language is limpid, uncluttered; each line often a unit of sense, a clear foil for the aural underpinning of the logic, or argument, of its sonnet: rhyme, alliteration and assonance chime and fuse with unmistakable authority.

It seemed to me that I needed to hold onto, or recreate, that clarity, and cohesion, if I was to have any chance of capturing the bravado and enterprise of the sequence as a whole. These twenty four sonnets explore the way the imagination unlocks sensual pleasure; they enact, through form, an elusive reciprocity; they reclaim ring-fenced areas of language and culture.

In short, Louise Labé rewrites the male Petrarchan tradition, giving it a blast of positive, debunking energy, a strong female voice and an intelligent physicality.

## Sonnet 16

When thunder and hail have beaten down a while
On high Mount Caucasus and its smoking thief
The day turns fair, dresses itself in light.
When Phoebus has blazed his ring around the earth
And speeding down into the sea, sinks back:
His sister rises, pointed diadem first.
Once the Parthian has fired his parting shot
He runs away, and lets his bow fall slack.

Seeing you cast down, I gave you consolation
Despite the sluggish flame of my own fire
But now you've fanned it, pressing consummation

And I'm at the point you wanted me most at
You've gone and doused your flame in water,
Are colder than I was, when you tossed your match.

## Sonnet 18

Kiss me again, kiss me, kiss me more:
Give me one of your most mouth-watering ones
Give me one of your most smouldering ones
I'll repay it with four, hotter than any embers.

Weary, you say? Here, let me find a cure:
I'll give you ten, all different, of rare softness.
Then as we mix up happiness and kisses
We two will please each other at our pleasure.

Now you and I will live our lives twice over
Once inside our self; once in our lover, and
Love, if I dare think this thought aloud,

Living in reserve makes me impatient:
How will I ever satisfy my ache,
Unless I rouse myself to seek, astride.

## Sonnet 19

Diana, finding herself deep in thick woods
Paused – having slain a raft of beasts –
To drink in cool air, garlanded by nymphs.
I walked, deep in thought, as I often do

Barely taking care: when I heard a voice
Call out to me: Clueless nymph, Diana
Is further in, you've lost your way. Curious,
Seeing me without bow or quiver, she asked

What did you encounter, friend, on your path,
Who has stripped you of your arrows, your bow?
I was stirred to action, I said, by a man who passed,

At him I desperately fired my arrows, the whole
Lot and the bow after. But he just picked them up
And shot them back, piercing a hundred holes.

## Sonnet 20

Someone once foretold that there would be
A man – and they described his face so I
Could see it, clear as the hour when it came –
Who would, one day, unshakeably, love me.

But seeing him fall in love so inevitably
Made me take pity on his doomed adventure,
I even forced and chivvied my own nature
Until I loved him back as passionately.

Who'd have thought this offspring of the joining
Of Heaven and the Fates, could do other than thrive?
But when I see such sullen clouds gathering,

Such bitter winds and such spiteful storms: I
Can't help thinking some remote infernal decree
Must have ordained this shipwreck, of you, and me.

# CHRISTINE DE LUCA

## *Arne Ruste in Shetlantic*

Arne Ruste holds a special place in contemporary Norwegian poetry. Since his debut in 1973 he has been a distinctly sensual, image-rich poet. His poems are immediate and warm; rich in knowledge of human attachment to religion and history, nature and landscape. *Kretsløp* (2012) is a fine 'New and Selected' collection from Tiden. He is an expert in rendering the big concerns of existence into apparently simple poems, often with reference to the natural world of which he is a keen observer.

Ruste and I have enjoyed mutual translation of our poems over the last decade, using English as a bridge language but, in both cases, keeping a keen eye on the Norwegian or Shetlandic as there are many similarities of sound and rhythm.

The English versions of these two poems were made by Olav Grinde, who lives in the US. Interestingly in 'Welcome' he shifted Ruste's Byens terminal (the city terminal in Oslo) to Grand Central Station in New York. I used Kings Cross where a Scot coming off the London train can feel strangely foreign. The poem fell into Shetlandic reasonably effortlessly: some words like *overstadig* translate easily into Shetland's *owresteer* (rather excessive behaviour) but perhaps the line *spraglete utenlandsk og fremmed nå* is the closest *spricklit, ootadaeks fock, fae fram noo*. Quite distinct from the English 'foreign and strangely speckled'.

The coming of Spring is a frequent theme for poetry but Ruste's 'Robin' is particularly apt and endearing. Some phrases like 'perplexed polyphony' and 'pubertal' have no direct Shetlandic equivalent so I had to take a tangential approach to get at the core of meaning (*cabbi-labbi* and *yallicrack* are somewhat onomatapoeic; and the phrases *filsket scriechin* and *slippit onkerry* hopefully embody the rather gauche physicality of youth). By way of balance there are other words and phrases where the Shetlandic and Norwegian share a sound quality or rhythmic similarity, particularly the final line.

Photograph © Dawn Marie Jones

## *Wylcom*

An dan der stirleens
in a stowin dunt
Da muckle oak is foo o stirleens
Kings Cross

Bön aa owre, new notts i der trots,
spricklit, ootadaeks fock, fae fram noo

– wi sun apö fedders
an waarm vowels
a speechil birthday

But i da haert o dat mird, aa his lane,
sporrow
een o da aald baand,
screchin full-trapplt

Owre-steer
glafterit or mad swaerie-wirds
hit's aa da sam

Geng du, peerie speug!

(CDL)

| ENGLISH (BRIDGE) | NORWEGIAN (ORIGINAL) |
|---|---|
| *Welcome* | *Velkomst* |

| | |
|---|---|
| And suddenly there are | Og så er det stær |
| starlings | plutselig |
| The big oak is full of starlings | Den store eika full av stær |
| Grand Central Station | Byens terminal |
| | |
| Well-travelled, heavy accented, | Verdensvant gebrokkent, |
| foreign and strangely speckled | Spraglete utenlandsk og fremmed nå |
| | |
| – with feathers catching the sunlight | – med sol i fjærene |
| and warm vowels | med varme vokaler |
| An extra birthday celebration | En fødselsdag på si |
| | |
| But in the midst of that flock, one solitary | Men midt i skokken en enslig |
| sparrow | spurv |
| one of the old faithful, you can hear him | av de trofaste gamle, for full |
| squalling full-throated | og skrålende hals |
| | |
| Excessively | Overstadig |
| joyful or angrily cursing | begeistret eller fly forbanna |
| doesn't really matter | kan være det samme |
| | |
| Carry on, sparrow! | Heia spurven! |

(OG)

## Robin

Yallow-trappled warbler,
gairden warbler, mavis,
jaunty blackie, spricklit
stirleen an snappy flycatcher; a chorus,
a cabbi-labbi, a yallicrack,
an if truth be telt, kinda lippened
dis filsket scriechin, dis slippit onkerry,
while we wait apö da cuckoo
i da trang haert o wir voar
noo an dan harkin
for da wheest whan der sittin

But suddenly der a vimmerin
a peerie mövment
i da bushes an trees,
aff a leg an on a leg
flittin fae branch ta twig ta spade-heft
ta mossy steyn,
apö meek fit,
apö cannie wing

An dan der robbie-redbreist,
red-trapplt, come
back again,
flitterin peerie-wyes
fae branch ta branch

## Robin

*(Erithacus Dandalus rubecula)*

Icterine warbler,
garden warbler, song thrush,
sanguine blackbird, speckled
starling and snappy flycatcher; a chorus
of perplexed polyphony,
and truth be told rather trite
this pubertal roaring of the senses,
while we wait to hear the cuckoo
in the midst of our busy spring gardening
sporadically listening
for the quiet
when they're brooding

But suddenly there's a light
motion, a gentle movement
in the bushes and thicket,
cautious shifts
from branch to twig to the handle of
the shovel to a mossy stone,
on meek feet, on
wary wings

And then there is robin,
red-throated, returned,
quietly moving
from branch to branch

## Rødstrupe

Gulsanger,
hagesanger, måltrost,
sangvinske svarttrost, spraglete
stær og fluesnapperen; et kor,
en fortumlet polyfoni,
temmelig fortersket, sant å si,
det pubertale bruset i sansene,
mens vi venter på gjøken
midt i onnestria,
og sporadisk lytter
etter rugestillheten

Men plutselig, en lett
rørelse, en nett bevegelse
under busk og kratt,
forsiktige
flytt fra gren til kvist til spadeskaft
til mosesten,
på saktmodig fot,
på varlig vinge

Og så er det robin,
rødstrupen, som er vendt
tilbake
og forflytter lydløst
fra gren til gren

his wine-red flag, wan laef
fae da hidmist hairst, liftit
bi a baff o wind, a brave haert
in sherry-coloured breist, an dat
pricks oot unseen boondaries
rings his hametoon
o wheest.

Ta ken, aal o a sudden,
dat hit wis dis, jöst
dis we waitit apön

*robin, inklin*

Robin, robbie-redbreist
i da callyshang o coortin,
Amontillado-breistit,
a banner flittin peerie-wyes
trig-lik an half-hoidin him
atween branches, aald
laefs, new buds
tracin his territory
o silence;
wan mintie, first
sure
inklin o voar

(CDL)

its wine-red flag, one leaf
from last fall lifted
by a wind gust, and this brave heart
in its sherry-coloured breast, who
stakes out the invisible boundary
around its domain
of silence.

To know, suddenly,
that it was this, just
this we waited for

*robin, sign*

Robin, red-throat
in the midst of the noisy nesting season,
Amontillado-breasted,
a banner carefully and
precisely moved, discreetly
between branches, old
leaves, new buds
tracing up its territory
of silence;
one small, the very first
reliable
sign of spring

(OG)

sit vinrøde flagg, et løv
fra i fjor, løftet omkring
av vindblaff, et modig hjerte
i sherryfarget bryst, og som
prikler ut usynlig stakitt,
ringer inn sitt rom
av stillhet.

Vite, plutselig,
det var dette, bare
dette vi ventet på

*rødstrupe, vink*

Robin, rødstrupen
midt i hekkelarmen,
amontilladobryst,
en vimpel forsiktig,
avmålt forflyttet, diskret
mellom grener, gammelt
løvverk, nye knopper
stipler opp sitt revir
av stillhet;
et lite, det første
tilforlatelige
vink av vår

# RĀBIʿAH AL-BAṢRĪ

In a version by Clare Pollard

Rābiʿah al-Baṣrī was an eighth-century Sufi mystic. Tradition has it that her caravan fell into the hands of robbers, who made her into a slave. She would perform her arduous tasks and then stay awake all night in prayer, and her master – on witnessing this – realized it was sacrilegious to keep her as his servant, and set her free. After this she became an ascetic, whose only possessions were a broken jug, a rush mat, and a brick she used as a pillow. She turned down numerous marriage offers, instead becoming a respected teacher with many disciples. Rābiʿah al-Baṣrī is considered the first Sufi to have set down the doctrine of Divine Love.

I discovered a handful of her poems last year in the excellent *Islamic Mystic Poetry* (ed. Mahmood Jamal). I found them really compelling in their razor-sharp purity – my first thought was of Sappho or Emily Dickinson. And so, as usual these days, I began to trawl internet bookshops and blogs looking for more. Although she is highly respected in the Islamic world (she's apparently been the subject of several movies in Turkey) the only other things that I could find in English were fragments – random quotations, unaccredited (Google?) translations on new-age sites, etc. It soon became clear that she wrote nothing down, so all lines attributed to her are fragmentary and doubtful anyway, but many of the scraps still contained something so interesting that I collated them, and started work on these new versions. They reveal a side of Islamic culture very different to that portrayed by the western media – Rābiʿah al-Baṣrī was a revered female philosopher and saint who, in direct contrast to fundamentalists, questioned everything.

## Lines after Rābiʿah al-Bsaṣrī

◆

In love there is nothing
between heart and heart.

Words ache after truth.
Only tasting is knowing –

an explanation is a lie.

How can you describe
the thing that wipes you out
and is you
and tells you what to say?

◆

If I bow because I fear hell,
burn me in hell

and if I pray for paradise,
lock the door of paradise

but if I love you for yourself,
let me look at you.

◆

My soul is a shrine,
mosque or church
where I kneel
at a blank altar.

Love is the place
of powerlessness,
of blazing loss –
rapture pours into itself,
its own drain;
its wings beat me
brainless,
bodiless.

I am a shrine,
a mosque, a church
that dissolves, that
is eaten by
God.

◆

In one hand, a flame,
in the other, water.

I am torching Heaven,
extinguishing Hell.

It is time to tear this veil down
and see the real God.

◆

Take the badness
mixed up in this prayer –
or take my prayer, badness and all.

◆

Death is the most intimate act.

Knowing who I'll kiss when it comes,
I consent to a thousand deaths.

◆

Sisters,
I recommend reclusion.
With my beloved
I'm peaceful,
nothing human
can compare –
he is where I struggle
and turn
and if I die of desire
and have not satisfied
my love,
well, poor me –
he is the craving and the cure,
existence, ecstasy...
I'm shunning all
this being for
the melting point –

# BHASKAR CHAKRABORTY

Translated by Manash 'Firaq' Bhattacharjee

Bhaskar Chakraborty is a poet who hears and writes silences. There is a ghostly ambience in his poems that reverberates with a strange depth, where the obscure is familiar and the familiar, obscure. Like almost all other poets from Calcutta, Bhaskar is a poet of the city, but unlike them, Bhaskar does not grapple with the sweat and toil, the hustle and bustle, of city life. He breathes and walks a different time, where the city is transported into memory. Calcutta is Bhaskar's nostalgia and nightmare. The absence of sentimentality in the poems adds to the emotional maturity of the poet's engagement with the city. Bhaskar is an imagist, and his poems constantly offer surprising and even shocking juxtapositions of imagery. It creates the strange ambience of his poems, where intimacy is often struck by unfamiliarity. His poems are also a constant conversation with death. It is crucial to read Bhaskar through the state of his illness, and the hallucinatory element it adds to his poetry.

## Winter

Your hair is flying in the air – in your left hand you hold
Your telephone
In the light of winter, I have again come to your room
I see your cat; it isn't as lithe as before –
The power of your fur; I see it go rolling – rolling
Beneath the tilted bed –
I sit quietly – your cat yawns quietly
The fountain of winter repeatedly calls us and recedes

## From Life

I had no idea, life would end like this, be spoilt like this. On days
only meant for roaming, I used to see the double-decker bus
swimming and rushing through Calcutta – in parks and restaurants,
boys and girls are floating and kissing each other. I had a colourful
shirt in my boyhood. I had a river veiled from life that sang the song
of eternal life. I used to think I had thousands of happy days – I used
to think I wasn't born to die just like that... Someone on top of the
hill has rolled a huge stone down over my life... I now see from inside
a broken train, black clouds have massed over my head, and water
from that old river is crashing over the many boats tied to my bed –
'Float, float, float away' – as I return silently to my little house.

## Illness

Did I desire the increasing presence of friends
By my bedside,
Ash falls from the cigarette at dawn
I need to do something
This lying and sitting down, this aimless wandering
Would it be good for me to move away
From a draught of wind
Did I want life to be ornate
From a dry window, the light of dawn is falling
On an empty pair of shoes
Did I want all that, brother
Did I want this

# WANG WEI

Translated by Ned Denny

This remake of Wang Wei's famous sequence of short poems was done several years ago as an experiment in what might be termed anagogic or hieroglyphic translation (by hieroglyphic I refer to the true function of sacred writing, whereby an image and its associations are allowed to resound in the mind – centrifugally but not arbitrarily – like the ripples of a stone thrown into a still pond). Another way of characterizing this approach would be to speak of an instinct for transcendence, something quite natural in people not subject to a process of systematic distraction. I made use of several English renderings – including G.W. Robinson's excellent Penguin Classics version – and a poet's audacious and perhaps unerring ignorance to produce something that may be closer 'to the cosmic bone', as Frank O'Hara said of Léger, than more correct versions. Or maybe not. The fidelity that concerned me was to what I feel and know and dream in my own bones, however obscurely, and also to the absolute solitude and perilous leisure that is both the curse and source of power of any genuine poet or free human being. My hope is that something of this perennial spirit, remote from both atheist and religious dogmas, has been evoked here. An occasional literary or cinematic allusion parallels the typical T'ang incorporation of fragments of classic poems, songs or chants, the one explicit borrowing being from Dylan Thomas's 'Poem On His Birthday' ('psilocybin' in that same section referring to the liberty cap or magic mushroom, which fruits like the bramble in late summer and early autumn).

# Wheel River

*after Wang Wei*

**I**

We have made our residence on the brink,
where the willow is living and dying.
Grave scholars who read us will never think
that the dead inherit everything.

**II**

Birds take themselves off into the stillness.
October glows as if painted on glass.
I stroll up the hill with my loneliness,
secure in the knowledge that nothing lasts.

**III**

The hazel's lichen-freaked trunks are my walls.
My great leaf-roof whispers God's hundredth name.
Alive in the woods, I cook up a storm
that will whirl to the cities. A real rain.

**IV**

Arterial trees reflecting in waters
hang downwards, suspended over a void:
we are dark heaven's thin sons and daughters,
rooted in soil we strive to avoid.

V

Country so deserted it seems crowded.
The lack of conversation fills my days.
In the shady depth of the mothering glen
are moss hairs lit by the sun's close gaze.


VI

The day gives the crisped hills a last caress.
A skein of geese undulates through the sky.
Here and there, an evergreen like a fire.
The clouds descend but find no place to rest.


VII

Come visit me. It's psilocybin time,
the brambles hold their black constellations.
We can groan in night-long ruminations,
getting 'lost in the unknown, famous light'.


VIII

In the tunnel of this overhung path
the starred moss deepens its luminous pile.
I pick up every stone I see, while
there's still a chance some pretty feet might pass.

## IX

I dream I am sailing into the sky.
The clouds clear and another Earth is there,
a pavilion where we sit together.
We can hear nothing but the butterflies.

## X

Satellites scan the world's inhuman shores.
The mind's antipodes are still unknown,
but no boat will make that crossing. Alone,
you must step into the sea-monster's jaws.

## XI

A melody blows us over the lake.
We call goodbye in the growing dark.
When I turn, the clouds have a dragon's face.
Entirety smoulders in every part.

## XII

At the palace, the pavements and coiffeured trees
would quickly drive me to despair. Out here,
I stray through a withered chaos of leaves
where everything's in perfect order.

### XIII

Streamlets like schoolchildren hurry down rocks,
the rain spits in my face, the bare wind sings
something I can't catch. In a dream, I watch
white egrets ascending and descending.

### XIV

You can take your monatomic gold,
your organic wheatgrass (locally sourced!),
your chicken soup for the insatiable soul.
To live forever, just drink from the source.

### XV

Another dream: I'm with Walt Whitman,
we are standing in a broad stream's shallows.
His ankles pale, that loneliest of men
is telling me the secret names of the stones.

### XVI

An object hums above the forest,
a shining sphere with no rivets or seams.
When I come to my senses, my mind clean,
I find I can't account for several minutes.

## XVII

Compose in darkness: yes. My eyes are clear
enough to discern a world's death-rattle.
I'm so far out, I'd be invisible
was it not for the moon's closed-circuit stare.

## XVIII

I think of Chuang Tzu, the idiot's post
that was the only job he'd ever had;
he fields another call, keeping a tab
on the tragic gestures of the willows.

## IXX

In late December, the wrecked wood flowers.
Everything opens, unfurls its light
in the disused mansion at the river's side:
our strange faces, the tips of our fingers.

## XX

We have emptied these hands and cupped our minds,
made a salad from the garden's choicest leaves,
left milk in saucers, tasted the breeze,
hailed the thunder. Now let the lightning strike.

# THE GREAT FLIGHT

*Refugee focus*

# RIBKA SIBHATU

Translated by André Naffis-Sahely

Ribka Sibhatu's poem was based on the real-life events of the night of 3 October 2013, when a boat of migrants from Libya sank off the coast of the Italian island of Lampedusa. The boat had many Eritrean and Ethiopian passengers on board. Ribka met with one of the survivors and wrote this poem in Italian as part of her activism on behalf of refugees from East Africa and elsewhere. In exile from her native country for over thirty years, Ribka has become one of Eritrea's most prominent voices. The poem was read out on Italian state radio in June 2015.

## In Lampedusa

On 3rd October
a barge carrying 518 people
arrived in Lampedusa
    Having survived a brutal dictatorship
    and a journey full of pitfalls
    they stood atop their raft in the dead of night
    and saw the lights of the promised land
Believing their suffering had reached an end,
they raised a chorus and praised the Virgin Mary.
While waiting for those ships to rescue them,
men and women, children and grownups,
the sick and the healthy began to sing hymns!

    ስምኪ ጸዊO መዓስ ሓፈሩ፡
    I wasn't ashamed when I called out Your name,
    ማርያም ኢለ ኣበይ ወዲቐ:
    I called out to Mary and didn't fall

ሰምኪ እየእ'ም ስንቄ ኮይኑኒ:
   Your name sustained me throughout my journey
እንሆ ምስጋናይ ተቐበልኒ!
   and here is the grateful echo of the song I raise to thank you!

Suddenly the raft
started filling with water;
they began flashing
red lights to sound the alarm;
switched their lanterns on and off!
Alas, all was quiet on the island.
Meanwhile the water rose, stoking fears the ship would sink.
   To send a distress call,
      they set a sail on fire, and as the flames
      began to spread, some frightened people
      jumped overboard and tipped the boat.
They were all adrift in the freezing sea!
Amidst that storm, some died right away,
some beat the odds and cheated death,
some who could swim tried to help
some drowned using their last breath
to send messages back to their native land,
some called out their names and countries of origin
before succumbing to their fate!
   Among the floating corpses
      Mebrahtom raised a desperate cry
      *Yohanna! Yohanna! Yohanna!*
But Yohanna didn't answer;
all alone, and in
an extreme act of love,
she brought her son into the world,

birthing him into the fish-filled sea:
yet nobody in Lampedusa
heard the seven ululations welcoming his birth!

      ሸሸሸሸሸሸሸሸሸሸሸሸሸ

    Because after a superhuman struggle
    Yohanna died alongside her son,
    who never saw the light of day
    and perished without even...drawing his first breath!
A baby died
drowned in the salty sea!
The baby was born and died
with its umbilical chord still unsevered!
A woman died while giving birth!
368 people died! 357 Eritreans died!
    On 3rd October
    3000 feet from Rabbit Island,
    in the heart of the Mediterranean,
    a tragedy struck the Eritrean people,
    one of many they have endured.

The poets were still writing, often on sodden scraps of paper rescued from the flooding.

# FIVE ASSYRIAN IRAQI POETS

Translated by Jamie Osborn and Nineb Lamassu,
with Cambridge Student PEN

The Assyrians are an ancient people with a cultural history
dating back to the Assyrian Empire, 3,000 years ago and beyond.
They have lived in parts of northern Iraq, Syria and Turkey for
millennia, but during the last century of conflict in Iraq have
suffered repeated massacres and persecution.

In November 2014, Cambridge Student PEN held a reading to
mark the Day of the Imprisoned Writer. Following the reading,
Nineb Lamassu came to us to ask for help for his people, the
Assyrian Iraqis. They were the opposite of imprisoned, he said –
or if they were imprisoned, it was an imprisonment in fear. They
had been driven out of their homes by ISIS, and were living in dire
conditions in flooded refugee camps. They had lost everything in
a matter of hours. The poets among them had lost a life's worth of
books and manuscripts, resulting in intense psychological pressure.
Nineb told us of how one of his friends had been sitting in the corner
of his tent for weeks, without speaking.

The poets were still writing, often on sodden scraps of paper
rescued from the flooding. They felt their suffering was not
known to the world, and believed it was their role to represent that
suffering in poetry. With Nineb's help, Cambridge PEN secured
and translated the poems written in the camps, and held a 24-
hour solidarity vigil and reading of the poems in Cambridge.
Representatives of British, Iraqi, Turkish, Kurdish, Israeli, Persian,
even Brazilian and Trinidadian writing communities were present.
Simultaneously, the Syriac Writers' Union, the body for Assyrian
poets, held a reading of the poems in the original Aramaic, which
they were able to record and send to us, to screen in Cambridge.
Rawand Baythoon, the President of the Syriac Writers' Union, told

us, simply, that 'it has turned our sadness into happiness', to know that the poems had reached so far.

While the Assyrians are a Christian minority, the writers of the Syriac Writers' Union insist that their work is not intended to present a sectarian view, but is a cry of suffering from any and all victims of ISIS.

## ABDALLA NURI

### *The Great Flight*

Our name is the first wound

Rich and poor taking flight
Both in terror
Both under the same scorching sun

Moses did not leave his people
He led them to manna and died
Jesus didn't leave his cross
He rose with courage and humility

When bombs fell on our homes
They soaked our soil with blood
They dried the song in the throat
Of the singing birds

Where are we going with tearful eyes
And our homes marked with a thousand ن

Kahramanat, Afrodite, Venus...

I feared for you Baghdede
For wolves roamed around your neck
Now
Nothing remains in my town
But ruined roads with stray dogs and cats
Searching for food
To fill their stomachs
Nothing remains in our homes
But looters and rotting heads
Nothing remains
Everything destroyed
But the barn-roof sky
Will give birth to that dawn
Nineveh will return and
Life will enfold our villages again

NOTE: ن (nun) is the first letter of the Arabic word for 'Nazarene' and is used by ISIS to mark out Christian properties to be seized. Unlike Masihee (Christian), Nazarene is usually derogative and also implies that the Assyrians are not an indigenous people of Iraq and Syria, but originate from Nazareth.

## BAYDAA HADAYA

### Severed Lips

They have changed my identity.
I was an Assyrian from Baghdede,
And now I am a refugee.
Wherever I go in this country of mine
I am required to prove that I am a refugee,
A refugee in my own country!

I will utter my words as a woman of Baghdede.
I will breathe them into an Assyrian breeze
Finding its way to St John's Cathedral,
To check if the church is still intact
And the old people's textile offerings still hang on the cross.
But why
Did they empty my town of its people,
Scatter them, beneath the sky?
Now the bell of St. John's – without its cross –
Rings not to summon people to prayer
But to announce another death.
Birds no longer fly through my town,
Nor does water flow in its palms.
Incense no longer drifts from its churches.
The melody of its church bells
Is replaced with cries of lamenting mothers –
Whose lips they cut.
They severed their lips
To prevent them kissing the cross –

O, how they crucified Baghdede in front of its children.

# BARZAN ABDUL GHANI JARJIS

## *My Mother's Heart*

My mother cried without tears
When she saw my naked sister in the rain,
My mother stripped her heart
And covered my sister with everything she had:

Love.

If you were to look up my mother's heart in a dictionary
The definition would be:
Sadness and tears for a country,
Burden of five orphaned children,
And grief for a murdered husband.

Someone came into my dreams
And whispered a few words:
Whispers – of my mother, my sister and the soil of my town.
It was my father's voice,
Imploring me to return to the soil that embraces his bones
So it could embrace mine too.

Will I breathe in the breeze of my town again?
Will I drink from Tigris' waters again?
My soul hovers over my town
And my lips sing its songs.
My heart cries blood, and my soul
Runs like a madman,
Wishing an end to this, or to life.

## ANAS AOLO

### *My Beloved Baghdede*

Two eyes
Gaze with longing
One cries blood
The other, fire
Tears flood
Our eyes
And Baghdede is set ablaze.

When I dragged myself to abandon you
I pulled all the churches behind me
They followed me, tapped my shoulder
And asked me to return
To Baghdede
I replied
I have taken Baghdede with me
I carry it where it belongs
So that my heart throbs with its love.

Is this a nightmare or
Have I really fled my home
How could I have abandoned my memories.

Only now I realise
How heavy the crosses of your churches were
Oh how you carried everyone's sins.

The day I fled my town, my beloved...
Every day I believe you are next to me
But you have changed...

You were big
I touch your hair
My beloved you are still beautiful
You still wear scarves
But here you are small
And your scarves are tents.


## AMIR POLIS IBRAHIM

### *The Crucifixion of Baretle*

My town was
Bound on the cross
They cut off its breast
(I suckled from there).
    It didn't cry.
They violated its purity.
    It did not cry.
But my town cries blood
For its displaced children
And we cry blood for its love.

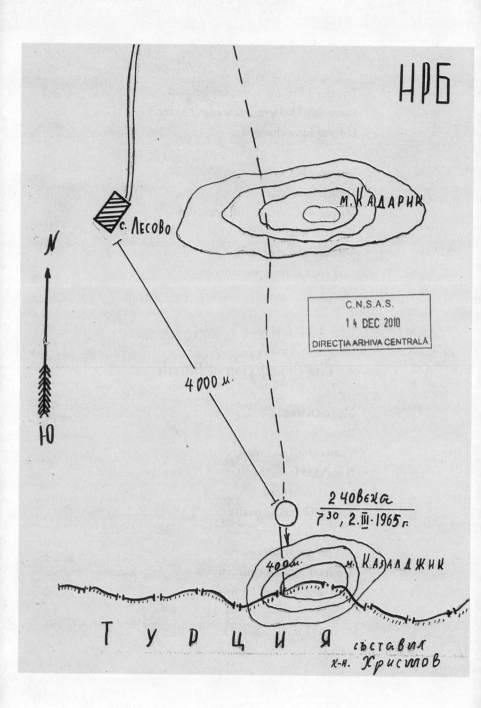

# CARMEN BUGAN

In October 2013 I took my father, mother, sister and brother on a journey back in time to our Romania. By that time I had read a good part of my family's secret police archive which I received from the Centre for the Study of the Archives of the Securitate (CNSAS) in Bucharest. Our family surveillance began in 1961 with my father before he was married, and ended (rich with material on the rest of us) when we emigrated to the US in 1989. Among the documents I had found a hand-drawn map of my father's failed escape at the border between Bulgaria and Turkey in the Lesovo area in February 1965 (see opposite). By 2014 my father was 79 years old and I wanted not only to trek the map made by the border guards but also to follow the map of his memory, the map of his face as he relived his story. I wanted to make together another map: the map of a journey as a free man. The poem 'A Walk with my Father on the Iron Curtain' came out of that experience.

## A Walk With My Father on the Iron Curtain

Arm in arm, my father and I return
to the ground of his failed escape:
it is now forty-eight years on.

The border between Romania
and Bulgaria at 110-111 point
is bathed in gold October light.

The maize silos where he slept are still here:
an old border guard curious to see us
loitering on the train tracks confirms Dad's memory,

as if History itself sent him our way
with the flock of geese and the red tractor
raising all the clamour in the peaceful morning.

It's a holy day for me, at my father's side,
with the map of his life, listening, listening
to the tempest in that night, icy rain, snow,

him and his friend inside the maize shelter
melting snow for tea, the horrifying days
when they searched the way with binoculars.

He ran to the other side of the world
with seventeen half-slices of salami,
a flashlight, and a dictionary,

some coins, probably more for good luck
than for anything they could buy, the shaver
for good looks, and a heart full of hope.

We carry on past Negru Voda:
Tolbukhin railway station, golden afternoon
and a wind that buffets us,

then Elhovo that looks more like a painting
with a dream worked inside the peeling blue
walls of the train station, my father, a puzzle

in changing light, seen through broken windows,
the coffee and baklava on the main street.
Arm in arm in the old quarters searching for his hotel

where he hid from police, the trap door that is
no longer there. Memory leads us off the map.
Then Lesovo in fog, like an elusive fish, the map

with the haystack where he slept to hide
from border guards, his hike along the roads
through the circular swamp, 400 metres from Turkey!

Ground of being on his ground of escape.
You cannot take the dreams away from anyone who dreams.
'I never thought I'd be back here as a free man,' he says.

Here he is, the white in his hair, snowbells at temples,
the grey-green eyes, now wet, now dry, twinkling.
Locals watch us step off ghost trains at the disused station.

# AMARJIT CHANDAN

Translated by the author and Julia Casterton

Astoria, Oregon is the birthplace of the revolutionary Ghadar party formed in 1913 by workers from the Punjab to liberate India from British colonial rule. Back home in the First Lahore Conspiracy Case, 291 Ghadris were tried and sentenced: death for 42, 114 were transported for life, 93 awarded varying terms of imprisonment. No one appealed against the punishments. 'The Ghadar movement,' said O'Dwyer, Colonial Governor of the Punjab, 'was by far the most serious attempt to subvert British rule in India.'

## *Suchness – Memorial to an Unknown Immigrant*

*In my talk I will project a blank slide for the Ghadar memorial that I believe should be in Astoria, Oregon.*
*– Johanna Ogden, historian (Email 6th November 2012)*

This white patch framed by dark
　　　　is the memorial that exists only in the mindscape.

It is the surface too delicate to bear the weight of any colour.

It has no horizon – here the earth and the sky never meet.

It is the still that always moves.

It is the passport to the unknown with the true likeness of the alien
　　　　attested in fate's hand
　　　　　　　　with the stamp of no return.

It is the timepiece whose hands move backward striking the past
    the moment he left home with moist eyes on the future.

It is the prisoners' dream.

It is the mirror spread out, burnt with the light of hope.

In the daylight sky the moon hangs over the shadowless tree.

It is the crescendo of vowels
    the text with no consonants.

It is the last page of the book of life that caused his end.

The void after the film reel snapped.

The peace frozen.

Suchness.

(AC)


NOTE: *Tathatā* – suchness – in Sanskrit and Pali; *Shunya* – absolute
emptiness – is a key concept in Buddhist philosophy.

# A Punjabi Compatriot in the Barcelona Metro

When you looked
I thought the old man is eyeing me.

Are you on your own?
No body came with you?

I can't work now.
I'm not that old – just twenty-five plus.

Have been here for six years.
Half the years I spent standing making *rotis* in the oven in restaurants.
Money's God.
Many boys went mad and suicidal.
For future we've mortgaged today's comfort.

Bahawalpur and Barcelona are drifting apart day by day.
Home is an island floating in the vast ocean.

The sun of this city welcomes all.
Leave the fog of London, come and live here.

The metro stopped at the next station.

Getting off he sighed and said:
What an age to endure pains.

And disappeared making his way in the crowd.

(AC)

## In This Country

In this country the foreigner starts losing his memory
    the day he arrives.

He remains speechless in his own language.

The air around translates his silence into English –
It is snowing.
Dry leaves are falling.
The sea waves recede.
The river ebbs away.
The tea is getting cold.
Photographs are fading.

He wonders – one shouldn't be in this country.
He keeps on being a stranger here, and
He starts believing in other strangers.

A cog is broken from the wheel of time.
The gramophone record moves on with the needle stuck
    in one track.

In this country the foreigner does not know what he does
    all the time.
He remains unaware     lost in his thoughts.
He wears *maojay* Punjabi shoes with his 3-piece suit.

In this country the foreigner keeps on looking at the photo
    in his old passport
        and gets scared of his own image.

In this country the foreigner is surprised to realise that
　　the way back home is rather long
When lost in his hometown the moon shows him the way
It keeps on walking with him till the dawn breaks and he knocks
　　on his own door.

(AC / JC)

## There's No Escaping Memories

There's no escaping memories

I wish memories were swallows
That fly endlessly to nowhere

I wish memories were letters
You pick, read and put aside
Whenever you feel like

How I have yearned this city could be mine
These roads
These rain-soaked lights
　　could hide me in their arms
And I could forget my past.

Whenever I walk
The tapes of old songs littered on the streets
Entangle my feet
Whenever the aeroplane passes over my head
It lands deep in my heart

My heart sinks and wonders time and again
Why it came, where it was bound

The wings of years shrink
A mystery bird neither flies nor sings
But trembles on my mind.

If there's no respite
I'm afraid I'll go mad.

There's no escape from memories.

(AC)

# MAYA TEVET DAYAN

Translated by Rachel Tzivia Back

The poem 'My Sister' is taken from a collection of poems in which
Tevet Dayan addresses her deceased mother, and expresses her
loss as an existential experience of migration from the home her
mother used to be for her in this world. For the mourning daughter,
that existential exile was soon followed by an actual migration
with her family to Canada, where another layer of homelessness
and alienation was added to her writings. Tevet Dayan's poetry is
significantly influenced by the Hindu concept of rebirth as well as
by the Jewish biblical imagination of the mutual yearning between
the individual and God. The poem 'My Sister' is an exception
from such imaginings: in straightforward, short sentences, the
poet addresses her sister, her partner in the destiny of an exile, to
describe the North-America external landscape that surrounds them
and that reverberates an internal landscape of absence and
orphanhood.

## My Sister

Now we are refugees
from the life that once was
ours,
that abandoned us like slippery
ground beneath our dreaming
feet. Now
in this other land,
the horizon is clear and blue,
the northern winds muddle
our memories
like sightless flies
and sometimes for hours
we can turn our blind
gaze away
from the chair beside us,
remaining always empty.

# HABIB TENGOUR

Translated by Caroline Price

Habib Tengour's poems are spare and sharply focused, without
a superfluous word. In beautifully weighted and highly visual
language they convey the poignancy of exile, both cultural and
physical, the search for identity, man's ambiguous relation to place
and the past. Although Tengour moved to France with his family
for political reasons before he was a teenager, and has written
mainly in French, the Arab and Berber storytelling voices of his
Algerian childhood haunt his writing and I tried to keep their
presence at the forefront of my mind as I worked. These poems,
written in 2014, were performed at the 45th Poetry International
Festival in Rotterdam the same year; 'Time to Set Out' and 'Living
at a Distance' deal with Tengour's great preoccupying themes of
identity and exile.

## Time to Set Out

I don't know the place
At the mouths of which rivers?

I've heard that in your country
The dead visit when it snows
To calm the troubled dreamer

They speak a language of fire and stone
Drink out of chipped cups with the birds

I know they head towards the West
When it's time to leave

When the ashes in the hearth grow cold

Exile trains its machine gun
At the border you feel empty, completely drained
The form you have to fill in baffles you

By morning love is revealed in still water
An invitation to cross over

## Living at a Distance

Ghostly figures of our friends rise up in the streets
To remind us of the exact moment
When hopes crumbled to a dust
Pierced from all sides by sun

We meet them in the padlocked bar
Of the fish factory in happier times
The judge and the grass rubbing shoulders
Each with his own crate on the table

They're an embittered bunch
Legacy of a decade with nothing to chew on

Brightly coloured paper napkins
Make a rainbow of welcome in the star-spangled doorway

A disappointing evening despite the festive preparations

# THREE ETHIOPIAN POETS

Translated by Chris Beckett and the authors

These three Ethiopian poets, all tenacious fighters for democracy in their homeland, fled three successive regimes: first, Hama Tuma from Haile Selassie's absolute monarchy in the early 1970s; then Gemoraw from the brutal military/communist Derg which overthrew Selassie in the mid 1970s; lastly, Alemu Tebeje from the Tigray-dominated government which sacked the Derg in 1991 and still rules Ethiopia today as a one-party state.

Hama and Gemoraw are heroes of the 1960s and 1970s student movement, centred on Addis Ababa University. Haile Selassie allowed a certain leeway to student expression, as long as this stayed on campus. Gemoraw famously won the annual university poetry competition with his still much-loved poem 'Berkete Mergem' (Gift of a curse), but it proved too richly rebellious for the Emperor who attended the reading but walked out in disgust!

Gemoraw's journey since fleeing Ethiopia took him first to China (where the authorities deported him for writing about the anarchist novelist Ba Jin who had been disgraced during the Cultural Revolution), then to Norway and finally Sweden. Hama bases himself in Paris and Alemu in London, but like all exiles there is a sense when you meet them that they have never left their country, however far they go or however many languages they master – and they are all dedicated linguists, including, in Gemoraw's case, of Ge'ez, the ancient precursor to Amharic. What I love about them all is their passion, their fearless and reasoned protest, and most of all, their modest humour in the face of barbarity and injustice.

Photographs: Hama Tuma (top left), Gemoraw (top right), Alemu Tebeje (bottom)

# ALEMU TEBEJE

## Greetings to the People of Europe!

Over land and sea, your fathers came to Africa
and unpacked bibles by the thousand,
filling our ancestors with words of love:

*if someone slaps your right cheek,*
*let him slap your left cheek too!*

*if someone takes your coat,*
*let him have your trousers too!*

Now we, their children's children,
inheriting the words your fathers left behind,
our bodies slapped and stripped
by our lifetime presidents,

are braving seas and leaky boats,
cold waves of fear –
let salt winds punch our faces and your coast-guards
pluck us from the water like oily birds!

but here we are at last to knock at your front door,
hoping against hope that you remember
all the lovely words your fathers preached to ours.

(CB / AT)

# GEMORAW

## *For The Voiceless People*

Of all freedoms, speech is the first,
and it is the tongue which allows us
to voice our desires and our desiring.

If the tongue is tied down and cannot tell
what we feel, not only our flesh is tied,
but our soul. And if our fellow man
is tongue-tied, we must speak for him too!

If we find ourselves in a free country,
what is the use of freedom,
if we do not speak for the speechless?
Is it a crime to say I am their fellow man?

*your tongues are burning, your hunger is raging!*
*blame the drought!* say our Authorities.
But for all those whose voice is silenced,
and who cannot cry *help!* for themselves: cry *help!!*

(CB / AT)

# HAMA TUMA

## *Just a Nobody*

The dead man was no one,
just a man in tattered clothes,
no shoes,
just a coin in his pocket,
no id cards, no bus ticket.
He was a nobody,
dirty and skinny,
a no one, a nobody
who clenched his hand before he died.
When they pried open his fingers,
this nobody,
they found a whole country.

(HT)

## Of Guilt

The man ran after his fart
to slap it back
and erase the shame.
The stink lingers.
Today's love is tepid, almost cold,
won't dry a hankie,
no heat at all.
Time has subdued my countrymen,
they pass history twice and
leave no shadow behind.
The frog in the pond
laughed itself to death, the owl is blind.
In the Waldiba monastery, forever silent,
noisy festivities are held.
Time moves on grinding all,
changing all,
but the crocodile has no teeth
and the Ethiopian no guilt:
everyone's heart is lost.

(HT)

# MOHAMMED DIB

Translated by Madeleine Campbell

Although Mohammed Dib's first language is Arabic, he has always
written in French. There is no question regarding his command
of the language: of Dib's first volume of poetry, *Ombre Gardienne*
(1961), French surrealist Louis Aragon wrote 'je ne me trouve point
devant une poésie traduite, *les mots sont les nôtres, les miens*' (I do
not find myself before a translated poetry, *the words are ours, they
are mine*). Yet Dib's poetry betrays the perennial ambivalence of
a transcultural heritage, so that a sense of 'the other' permeates
his writing. Exiled to France in 1959, drawing deeply on Maghrebi
culture and Sufi mysticism, his poetics grew increasingly ascetic
and disorientating. His use of impersonal, indeterminate syntax
and diction intensifies this sense of *dépouillement* (denudation). He
received the Prix Mallarmé (1998) for *L'Enfant-jazz* (Jazz child). The
poems featured here are from the second of three sections in this
collection, which Dib introduced with the remark that poetry is 'là
où regarder s'appelle voir, c'est-à-dire dévisager au fond de soi ce
qui est devant soi' (where to look is to see, or to behold deep within
oneself that which stands before us). The prescient indeterminacy
of identity, place and agency in these poems heightens the urgent
sense that today's refugee crisis cannot be reduced to the plight
of particular ethnic or religious groups, nor to far-off regions, but
concerns everyone of us.

Permission for these translations has been graciously granted by
the publishers of the French language edition *Œuvres complètes de
Mohammed Dib, I Poésies* © Éditions de la Différence (2007).

## Day's End

They were coming. A day's
End when everything lingered.
They were coming, you could see
They had walked a long way.

Had abandoned many faces
On the road. A great many.
Do they even know where they are
Said the child. Do they know.

Now he too lingered
At the window. Night fell.
They walked past, even those
Who had lost a face.

The child looked away.
Pulled the window shut. They,
Said he, have gone. He knew.
He found the night inside again.

The same again and most of all
A sparrow flapping its wings.
A sparrow in here? Said he.
In agony here? Said he.

## Them

One of them walked past.
Things turned away.
There would be others.

Another walked past.
The trees held hands.
He saw this from the window.

And others came.
Through the glass panes
He merely saw the violence.

Or rather, he merely saw
Their white hair
Cut short at the nape.

Like flat polished stones,
Necks and vile faces, necks
And stares. A stare for a stare.

## The Strangers

They came so close. He stole
A glance. Would not forget.

What they wanted from him.
Motionless, they waited.

They exhaled softly.
Shrouding the silence.

# DON MEE CHOI

I was born in South Korea during the U.S.-backed military dictatorship. I grew up in a small, traditional house my father bought with his award money for his photographs of the Student Revolution of 19 April 1960 that took place in response to President Rhee's anti-democratic and dictatorial rule. What my father still remembers about the uprising is that many children, orphaned during the Korean War, gave up their lives because they had nothing more to lose. What I remember are the children, no older than me, who used to come around late afternoons begging for leftovers, even food that had gone sour. The drills at school in preparation against attacks by North Korea kept me anxious at night. I feared separation from my family due to the ever-pending war. I feared what my mother feared – my brother being swept up in protests and getting arrested and tortured. Our radio was turned off at night in case we were suspected of being North Korean sympathizers. At school, former North Korean spies came to give talks on the evil leader of North Korea. I stood at bus stops to see if I could spot any North Korean spies, but all I could spot were American GIs. My friends and I waved to them and called them 'Hello's'. In our little courtyard, I skipped rope and played house with my paper dolls amongst big glazed jars of fermented veggies and spicy, pungent pastes. I feared the shadows they cast along the path to the outhouse. Stories of abandoned infant girls always piqued my interest, so I imagined that the abandoned babies might be inside the jars. Whenever I obeyed the shadows, I saw tiny floating arms covered in mould. And whenever it snowed, I made tiny snowmen on top of the covers of the jars. Like rats, children can be happy in darkness. But the biggest darkness of all was the midnight curfew. I didn't know the curfew was a curfew till my family escaped from it in 1972 and landed in Hong Kong. That's how big the darkness was.

In 1980, my father filmed the rising waves of student protests against the dictatorship in Seoul. He also witnessed the beginning of the brutal military crackdown on the pro-democratic movement in Kwangju. He believed then that the dictatorship would not end and that it would be too dangerous for us to return home. He sold one of his cameras to pay for my older brother's surgery, who was injured during his mandatory military service. He gave the South Korean government news footage of a student protest in exchange for the release of my brother from the military and a permit to leave South Korea. He thought then that he was saving us from a life of perpetual darkness. In 1983, my family 'scattered all over', as my mother said. My parents and my younger brother headed to West Germany. My sister remained in Hong Kong, my older brother left for Australia, and I went to the US as a foreign student to complete my degrees in art. In light, we all ailed from separation and homesickness. In light, we had to find a way to settle down, as my mother said. In light, we lived like birds.

# GOLAN HAJI

Translated by Stephen Watts

Golan Haji wrote the first notes for 'A Light in Winter' at the Grand Palais retrospective of Bill Viola's work in Paris in Spring 2014. A few months later he reworked them into this poem in half-remembrance of the exhibition and halfway between the dream processes that perhaps video art and poetry share. These distances and ambiguities reflect quite naturally on the complex experiences of mirrored absence: both Viola's art and Golan's poem lend themselves to language on the edge of deflection and to the ability to meditate on the nature of 'exile' (a word incidentally that Golan Haji is very wary of being pigeonholed into).

I travelled to Paris in February 2016 expressly to co-translate more of his poetry, and 'A Light in Water' is one of the results of that happy journey. I'd met Golan at the Al-Sendian (Al-Mallajeh) Festival in Syria in 2010, a beautiful gathering of poets, artists, photographers, children and villagers, and the last of its kind before the appalling years of rupture exploded in 2011. Golan managed to leave Syria in 2011, first for Jordan and then to Paris, where he has lived since. We've translated his poems across the intervening years whenever there was an opportunity to snatch time to sit, or walk, together – this shared space being vital because it gives us the scope to directly test and coax the fluency, physicality, verve and edge of Golan's poetry into something not too dissimilar in English. When it works (and intuitively we feel it sometimes does) then 'a happy journey' is perhaps the most appropriate description of this dialogue of translation.

# A Light In Water

*Bill Viola sequence*

(Innumerable Attempts To Reach Eternity)

The simple but impossible method of achieving immortality is to stop breathing, then to stay alive without breath.

The dreamers are sleepers fully dressed under the water. Bubbles are a sign of life as of the body's decay. We can't be sure which. They sleep on the stage and their hands don't move, and the waves delude you into thinking that their fingers stir in weak and final motions.

An illuminated column writhes in deep waters, a young man's plunge as a comet swallowed by a whirlpool; we were in front of those waters and he didn't see us standing there, behind us the great conflagration. Bubbles, stars come up from the depths, were merging together, increasing in size as they surfaced towards us. We all are black shadows in this great night, unless the huge fire be damped down. No one will see us as long as such conflagration is behind us and no one will see us if we are inside it.

Did we go far or get close or will we melt soon? We heard the sea's roar in the desert, our faces were touched by hot air blowing through the windows of the cars we were crammed into. Immaculate brightness dazzled our eyes. Dry waves ascended like transparent tongues above flames beneath a burning sun. So this is a mirage! I love it neither as symbol or metaphor but as a phenomenon. I delight in being deluded by my eyes.

◆

(The Painting)

Among the body-parts, after death, the hand is what most resembles its bones.

You are not a documentary film. You are a painting. No events are happening here so don't expect anything. Inside the painting there is another painting and a faint ray of light passes through that frame to fall on a solitary book whose letters are tiny and wide open as your lungs. The same ray lights the knitting needle inserted by a woman into a skein of wool. A spider's thread shines on a potted cactus; there's no escaping fragility, there must be a breeze for you to see such tenderness in a thin thread that summarizes your destiny.

Very slowly the painting moves from screen to screen. The changes are slight. On the first screen the woman who disappeared is sleeping naked, that candles might be lit behind your eyes on another screen. Had you slowed down you would have seen all of this. Don't rush things. Don't be the one on whom slowness is forced, don't be the convalescent or the old man. Slow down exactly when you might be hurrying off. Put on your clothes without haste. Do everything in slowness. Perhaps you will find some sort of solution or hope.

The painting is still hanging on the same wall, and if you stretch your hand out towards the woman asleep inside there, you will see a hand slowly opening its fingers underwater.

◆

(The Screens)

Between the two screens there's a barrier that's like a threshold between the mirror and the world. On each screen a figure is

standing, holding himself together, breath-stopped in front of a
dark liquid, then the man in the red singlet begins to cry, and after
him the woman with the blue singlet starts crying too. Are they
runners, wanting to reach genuine tiredness after long exertion,
the tiredness of the body that silences the tinnitus of death? You
will not recognise a man sobbing in his solitariness. First you see
the reflection of his face distorted by his tears in the pitch dark of
water, then you see how these tears melt his face. No sounds are
audible. You are watching the strangled weeping of two people each
the shadow of the other, a man and a woman exchanging roles, each
entering the black mirror only to leave it the next time round.

Every face is a reversed mask placed on water. The nose and the
mouth are open but no one can breathe easily. Gasped-out, trapped
sighs are blown into the water: we can see bubbles but can't hear the
bubbling, and the gap between water and air is as narrow as that
between life and death, a barrier of two centimetres. We will always
see someone crying, standing surrendering themselves before water.

◆

(The Jump)

We saw him in the distance, naked. When he came close to us
we found that he'd dressed on the way. How that happened when
the land is so open we don't know. A man unknown to us, he has
remained here, whereas his physical movements were taking place
in parallel times. He stood for a long while at the edge of the water
without throwing himself in; he remained standing there lowering
his head and closing his eyes. But when he did jump his leap was
incomplete. He stayed held in mid-air as if transformed into an
image of a world suspended above water, whereas ripplings were

wrinkling its surface. This water on the earth, inside a square stone frame, is not a mirror; but a painting more ancient than us.

At this moment, the man is suspended in mid-air like a diver or a foetus, his body a ball, and nothing is holding him in place; around him small leaves and fruits are dropping from the beaks of birds that are flying above him, though we cannot see them. Maybe a sparrow is feeding its young a large butterfly whose wings are crumbling in its beak and the dust of the wings settles on the water's face and wrinkles slightly there.

Slow down. Had you looked longer you would see. Above the water it was night with a half moon and just a few stars, but high high up the air still had the light of day. Immeasurable time had passed through this stillness, before a weeping willow covered a man who tried to jump. Was he thinking to swim, or of death? We don't know. We don't know the depth of anything we see. In this quiet rustling, if you come upon thick leaves and branches that touch the water, try to look for the openings: there's someone we don't see, like this man who tried to jump; like a hand stretched out to a drowning man, his shadow trembling over the face of the water, and little by little it entirely vanished. What remained were the soil, the water and the trees.

◆

(Meandering Ones)

They take off their phosphor helmets and their coarse gloves, and lean their backs against the rocks in the evening. They've tied the chains back on the cranes, and with animal shears they cut the ropes of the hanged, leaving a woman alone, praying at the edge of water, her arms folded and her hair white.

Everyone realized that speech was unnecessary. The rescue crew and construction workers are on stage and their theatre's in front of ancient trees beneath a cloudy sky, but the crowd becomes bored and ambles on, thinking that nothing's happening here.

We travel to look back. We travel and we look back and we still see the quiet file that has been moving slowly through the forest behind us since dawn. Are those the same people who go back and forth rehearsing the same scene? Are we hypnotized by repetition? It's daytime now and you gently pass your fingers over the forehead of the sleeping woman kissing her as if consoling someone who is dying, your slow motion all tenderness.

You knock a long time on the door of a dying man you left alone a short while ago, lying on his old marriage bed. You are listening out for his breath but you hear nothing. You keep listening until it's your own breath you hear and it's death knocking on the door of your heart; and if the door is opened you will not see the waxen face or toothless jaw. Someone has locked the door and thrown the key in the great water and left. A cab that had been waiting for him in front of the entry stairs took him away.

A grandfather clock resembling a big wooden headstone, its two hands still rotating, tolling its bell for midday. A river gull perches on its crown. The old man and old woman are sitting on two chairs, close by their things that fill the boat that's sailing away now, their bedroom mirror between them. Their house is sailing off with them inside it, crossing the great water slowly. We, who always watched them from our balconies and windows, are left behind, as if we were the dead.

(The Deluge)

You don't notice anything because you see like someone who
remembers.

Like a prophet in a film, be the camera.
Meanwhile the entire city passes by: on the sidewalk a homeless
man holding a piece of cardboard 'I am hungry'. The benefactor, the
preacher, and the one who pities approach him, but in the end it's
an air hostess who accompanies him beyond your field of vision. A
lady carrying an orange tree crowned with just a few oranges passes
by, another lady walking cautiously and carrying a large china bowl
passes by, and more than once the same man carrying books balanced
between his hands and his chin, he's elderly and bald with round eye
glasses. Men with hoardings pass by, a lady carrying an empty cat
basket, a man carrying a large maquette of a house, and behind him
a small girl wearing shoes larger than her feet and carrying a bear
doll. A lady pushing a pram containing a bonsai pine, a small child
whose red balloon bursts in front of him. And a large rolled-up carpet
carried by two wall-painters. A young woman descending the stairs
and remembering, before leaving the building, that she'd forgotten
something and you understood it was her black bag. Many bags pass
in front of you, some people clutch one in each hand. Someone who's
carrying a cheap chandelier, a lady whose shopping bag has burst and
a young man helps her to gather her spilt groceries before quickly
leaving. People arguing and shouting without noticing you're there. A
tall girl opening her parasol for her less tall mother, a group of women
in mini-skirts whose calf muscles are strong, men who look back as if
their pockets might have holes, a priest carrying a box with a parrot

in a cage tied on top. Someone who's carrying a column of grey hats and another who's carrying a television and a third carrying a heavy blanket in a transparent bag. Then you see most of those who have passed in front of you returning from the opposite direction, doing the same things, everyone acting as if the porter of their own lives. Are those who were in a rush the same ones who escaped with their skins? Has all this scene been taking place in a mirror? What is the difference now between the original and the copy, the image and its reflection, sleep and wakefulness? Don't leave, illusion. What does it matter if the deluge comes.

# MAJID NAFICY

Translated by Elizabeth T. Gray, Jr.

Majid Naficy was born in Isfahan, Iran, in 1952 and currently
lives in West Los Angeles, California. Raised in a large and well-
educated family, his first poems were published in a literary journal
in Isfahan when he was just 13. After studying at the University of
California at Los Angeles, Naficy returned to Tehran University,
abandoned writing poetry, and joined political groups working to
overthrow the Shah. After the 1979 Revolution, when Khomeini
began to crack down on dissidents, Naficy and his wife, Ezzat
Tabaiyan, were forced to go underground, but continued to work
against the new regime. In 1981 both Ezzat and Naficy's brother,
Said, were imprisoned and executed and thereafter, in 1983, Naficy
fled the country. With the help of Kurdish guerillas, Naficy escaped
to Turkey on horseback, carrying the nine poems he had written
after Ezzat's death, some money, an Afghani passport, and torn
photos of his brother and wife. Eighteen months later he was
granted asylum in the U. S. and moved to Venice, California.

Naficy's poetry has been widely anthologized, and he has
published more than twenty collections of poetry in Persian and
two collections in English. He is a beloved poet among Iranian exiles
in Los Angeles and elsewhere, and an inspiration to many. In his
honour, a stanza of his poem 'Ah, Los Angeles!' is engraved on the
wall of a city park in Venice.

These two poems of Naficy's speak to two poles of exile: the
longing to return to a fondly remembered homeland and the desire
to sever ties with an old life and build anew in a foreign land.

# One Night I Will Return to My Birthplace

One night I will return to my birthplace
to stand on my rooftop
and pick stars.

Father will say, 'Look, There!
Don't you see the Seven Brothers?'
I will stretch out my hands
and caress their unsheathed swords.
Then the nightly battle will begin.
Together we will cast out the moon-eating dragon
and in the dark corners of heaven
we will fasten each star firmly in place.

At dawn Mother will say, 'Look,
There! Don't you see the Two Sisters?'
I will stretch out my hands
and caress their jugs of water.
They are the messengers of the rain-making clouds
that disappear with the rising sun.

My brothers! My sisters!
One night I will return to my birthplace
so that under my childhood sky
I will find again my own stars.

NOTE: The 'Seven Brothers' refers to the Pleiades, and the 'Two
Sisters' are the dog stars Sirius and Procyon.

## To Iranians in Exile

When will we burn our ships?
It's been a long time since we dropped anchor in this harbour.
The sea's storms have nested in our souls,
our hands have not yet let go the heavy lines
and our eyes see nothing but the whiteness of salt.

Death has been mixed with our saliva
and no mouthwash can make our mouths pure.
Greedy mice chew on our memoirs
and their footprints cover the deck.
Birds no longer circle above the mast
and breadcrumbs
remind us of nothing at all.
It's been a long time since our spouses abandoned ship
and our children have been lost in the wailing wind.

Where is our fire-maker?
So that by striking a match
she can set our threadbare sails on fire
and open the way for the pure fire
to burn the ancient charts to ash.
Go on, let's leave the sea to the sea
and burn the travel story of Sinbad the Sailor.
On this hard shore we must stand
and feel the solidity of the ground beneath our feet.

Among us
can we not find a woman like Roma
to burn this ancient ship?
Tell her to rise up
and before the vultures
dance on our bodies
tell her to come
so that in the shining of her savage eyes
we may see the miniature Iran
that on the edge of these Pacific waters
will grow, little by little, from our hands.

NOTE: According to Plutarch's *Life of Romulus*, when the survivors of Troy arrived in Italy a woman by the name of Roma set fire to their ships, forcing them to give up the idea of returning home and thus to build the city of Rome.

# NASRIN PARVAZ

## *Writing in the 'Host' Language*

Over the years since I came to England in 1993 as a political refugee
from Iran, I've been to many fiction or creative writing classes and
seminars, where I was the only person who did not have English as
their first language.

The teachers and the other students always welcomed me and I
usually found the classes very helpful. It took me a while, but I began
to wonder why no other non-native English language speakers came to
these classes.

We all know London is full of non-native English speakers and
among them there are many writers. Some exiled writers are members
of organisations such as Exiled Writers Ink, who run readings
specifically for refugees or immigrants, but the majority of exiled
writers are working in isolation within their own communities; and
no matter how long they have lived here, most writers from immigrant
and refugee communities continue to write in their native tongues.

This last puzzles me, as while it is obviously easier to write in the
mother tongue, and of course each language has its own idiom and
beauty, English is the world's international language and writing in
English offers any writer a far larger potential readership.

It is true books can be translated into English but in practice only
three percent of all the books published in English are translations
from other languages. Writing in our mother tongues means we talk
to ourselves, not the world, and I will argue that this creates a cultural
apartheid, which suits the 'cultural colonisers'.

I write because I want to speak to the world, and that surely is
the reason all writers write and I wondered why other non-native
English speakers were denying themselves access to the wider world.
And then I questioned myself, were they in fact denying themselves
deliberately or were there other factors that I had not recognised (and

had somehow not experienced) which inhibit immigrant and refugee writers from trying to write in the *lingua franca*.

I began to look at the factors that maintain what I have called cultural apartheid. First (and this is controversial), our host country has no integration policy. The first move to integrate 'others' into British society would be to give newcomers access to free or very inexpensive English classes. Up until the early 1980s, this had been state policy, but slowly, both local councils and government moved from a policy of providing English classes to providing translators and interpreters. This has disempowered immigrant and refugee communities, as without real knowledge of the host language we not only have difficulty talking to our hosts, but we have difficulty communicating with different immigrant and refugee groups who speak in different languages. This policy of providing interpreters and translators rather than English classes disempowers, ghettoizes us and keeps us as the permanent 'other'.

Perhaps we stay in our ghettoes because we feel threatened and beleaguered and feel safer among 'ourselves'.

The Daily Mail, 17 November 2015, published racist cartoons, showing us as dangerous rats swarming into western countries, when we should be facing a closed door. Perhaps subliminally we can only write in our own 'ratty' languages, for our fellow 'rats'?

And that means, while we are vilified, we are also silenced. Our stories and insights into the human condition are shared only with each other. The host 'natives' continue to get their information about us from the mainstream media which is not interested in our struggles any more than it is interested in western complicity in the tragedy which has overtaken so many of our countries. Now in the current crisis the media attacks the easy target of 'people traffickers', but not the western politics which has created this huge movement of people.

And where are the Tolstoys who will write of today's War and Peace? Still writing in their own mother tongue, which the world will not hear?

Perhaps he or she died on their journey of escaping and never reached the ultimate exile to tell the story. And what about those who are able to bring the shell of their bodies to the shore of exile? There are so many 'foreigners' in every country, but they don't have a say. There are so many writers among them; yet they are not accepted in the host country as equal to a native writer. It seems the word 'exiled' means 'condemned'.

The struggles to have a voice force writers to escape execution and imprisonment and they end up in exile. In exile they can shout as much as they like, but no one hears them, because we are sectioned and we cannot reach people. Writers in exile, it seems, experience a censorship that is of a much more subtle order than that of their native countries.

So, while the immigrants' writers are held between the pain and safety of exile, they are also watched with suspicion. As if their writing in English might contradict the sameness of the white space. Or they might write about here and now, and that is not considered a subject for them to write about. So, despite the fact that it is usually the white bullet that we escape from, no matter if it is aimed at our heart by our government or by a white man through war, here it is not the white bullet that keeps us silent, but white racism through marginalization and dehumanization by mainstream media. It is in this order that we the exiled writers do not have a voice but in a different way from the way in which we had no voice where we were born.

Lack of integration policy and racism prevent immigrants and refugee writers from expressing themselves in English. However, it is not enough that here we can speak against our governments without facing persecution. We need to force our way into the society and try to have a voice in the world by writing in English about the injustice in every country. Only in writing in the world's international language can we reach the world and tell it what we fought for and why we must die in exile. And this might help the future generation to have a better life, by turning our individual struggle into one great movement for justice in the world.

# YOUSIF QASMIYEH

Translated by the author

> Upon being faced with a real world, one can discover in himself
> the being of worry. [...] Are there other nothingnesses than the
> nothingness of our being?
> – Bachelard, *The Poetics of Reverie*

The concept of 'the nothingness of our being' has become omnipresent
in an era where responding to a disaster via writing or, to follow in
Blanchot's footsteps, 'writing the disaster', becomes the correlative of
presence itself. The presence that is no longer measured through living
but more precisely by how life itself, in the presence of all these beings
who insist on moving to counter death, has become translucent, like a
fleshless body. But whose body is it? It is beyond a shadow of a doubt
that of the refugee. The body that conquers language, noise and, above
all, borders to hear itself en route.

These fragments, written by moving in and out of Arabic and
English, and at times, transposed and translated from Arabic into
English, claim nothing other than the fragmentary body of the refugee,
the corpus that is carrying its corpse and others.

## If this is my face, so be it

Walking alongside his shadow, he suddenly realised that it was both of them who needed to cross the border.

They fortified their walls with cement and nails. They moved their women and children to a safe place and shouted: they are coming after our faces; they are coming after our crops!

Immemorial is the smell of refugees.

*The body is but a wound.*
Nancy, *The Birth To Presence*
The equivalence of a refugee would be his body.

Wake! He said to his body when they arrived. A bit of air was in the air.

The child has become water... It is to the side, a tad clear, a tad not, but when you look him in the eye you will see the meaning of water.

Whoever can sense the coming is a refugee. The refugee can neither come nor depart; he is the God of gestures.

We might also say: the face is a dead God.

Whoever claims asylum, whoever lends his hands to his strangers so they could bear out his presence and his things, is the one who has many deities and none.

The incorporeal is the body of the refugee.

Refugees and gods always compete for the same space.

What is intimate is the face and never the refugee.

The refugee is only intimate in his death and if there is only one death to ponder, it is that of the refugee.

If this is my face, so be it. For once, it is a stone's throw away.

The immanent being is the refugee.

A being with cracked soles is Man.

They use their voice to 'sacrifice their sacrifice' (Derrida, *The Animal That Therefore I Am*).

The refugee is the superimposed being. Not only does he act as an alibi (to existence), he also creates existence. Without the refugee, existence is no longer existent.

Refugees, to kill time, count their dead.

Killing time is the correlative to killing themselves.

A no-place is what substantiates a deceased refugee.

A death with no place can never happen.

A refugee only returns to bear witness to his own return.

In the absence of time, arrival takes place.

Claiming asylum is the act of self-annihilation *sensu stricto*.

Claiming asylum always results in the overreading of the proper noun.

This happens when it is enough to say that it is the body that claims asylum. The body by itself. The body as its body. Whatever state it is in, it is the body, the body in the flesh, that submits itself in front of other bodies, in order, first and foremost, to be declared present, made present, or to be seen as such by those with more mature flesh and finer cuts. In the flesh, the refugee arrives while bearing witness to his own body, while holding the narrative of the body: I am sacrificing my body for myself; nobody and nothing else, to edge back into the ladder of bodies and be a sign amidst signs. The body is by itself; bare, melancholic as the body in its first outing. Whatever state it is in, it is that that carries all states to the threshold. To the borderline whose remnant is a body and whose body is a remnant. In the flesh is what the refugee can see with or without the gaze.

Only those who have never seen a place can describe the place.

Those who flee their homes tend to have faces that are slightly clearer than the moon. In the above clarity, only the face can substitute its creator.

Claiming asylum is a claim that can only be proven posthumously.

With the same limbs, raptors and refugees hunt for place.

In asylum, we borrow our bodies for the last time.

Whenever my mother wanted to leave the house, it was to see God's face. God's face, according to her, was somewhere else.

Man, how is it that your body is intact?

The refugee is he who fears himself. When the self is deafeningly mauled, he will fear the place but never the animal.

There is nothing sacred about the sacred save the eyes.

To claim asylum is necessarily the claim that no being can prove or otherwise.

Damned is the place. Damned is the one.

On the threshold, they slaughtered us and time.

# JUAN GELMAN

Translated by Keith Payne

On 14 January, having just returned from Mexico to Galicia's wettest winter in seventeen years, I was sat in the library in Vigo's old town when the news came down the wire that Juan Gelman had died. While the rain hammered the glass-domed roof of the Juan Compañel library, I read *Bajo la lluvia ajena*. These poems were part of Gelman's return to poetry after a four-year silence: 'I felt hatred for the military junta, I felt indignation, I felt powerless because I could do nothing in exile except denounce the military dictatorship, but nothing more. And that's why I wrote nothing for four years.' *Under the barbaric rain* are poems of the silenced exile, the exile whose jaw has been wrenched apart. The exile that you walk past on the Coal Quay in Cork City, the Rue Mouffetard in Paris or the Avenida de las Americas in Madrid. Exiles or migrants silenced by brutality and language. The literal translation of 'Under a distant rain' wasn't sufficient shelter for Gelman's migrant. 'Barbaric' suggested itself, with its brutality and inherent exclusivity of the safe native who can't or won't try to understand the migrant. There's a word in poem VII of the sequence; *asediaron*, meaning to besiege and containing the word for thirst, *sed*, as in to drive someone out by thirst as opposed to the French *sege*, simply to 'sit it out.' My original reading of the poem, under that pummelling rain, reminded me of the exile's last resort to the sup that often slakes his solitude. Yet here was Gelman 'unashamed of nostalgia' and forced to move through borders and languages. His poems migrated through the Lunfardo of his native Buenos Aires, then Spanish and Italian until he arrived at the Ladino of the Sephardim – that last great language of the migrant – that is, until today.

# Under the Barbaric Rain.

*An Excerpt*

I

It's difficult to reconstruct what happened, the truth of the memory battles against the memory of the truth. Years have passed, the dead and the hatreds pile up, the exile is a cow that can give poisoned milk, some are nourished by this [...]

The need to destroy yourself and the need to survive battle each other like a pair of crazed brothers. We hang up our clothes in the wardrobe, but we haven't yet unpacked the baggage of the soul. [...]

III

I won't be ashamed of my sadness, my nostalgia. I miss the back street where they killed my dog and where I cried beside his body, where I'm stuck to the pavement with my dog's blood as he died, I'm still alive since that day, it's what keeps me alive, it's what I am, and I'll ask nobody's permission to be nostalgic.

Maybe I'm different? There were military dictatorships, civil governments and more military dictatorships, they took away my books, bread, my son, they drove my mother to despair, they banished me, they assassinated my little brothers, they tortured my friends, they tore them to pieces, they broke them. No one removed me from the street where I am crying beside my dog. What dictatorship could do that? And what military bastard will remove my great love of the gloaming in May, where the soul's flight is balanced on the night?

My country, it wasn't perfect before the military coup. But it was mine, the times I trembled against love's barricades, the times I was a

boy, dog, man, the times I loved and was loved back. No general is
going to strip my country of all that, the land I watered with love,
with a little or a lot, land that I miss and that misses me, land where
no military will muddy my mind or leave its grime.

It's right that I miss her. We always loved each other like this: she
asking more of me, me asking more of her, both hurting from the
pain we inflict on the other, both strengthened by the love.

I love you, motherland, and you love me. That love smoulders
imperfections, lives.


09-05-1980


V


Of the exile's duties:
don't forget the exile /
dispute the language that disputes the exile/
don't forget the exile / that is the land /
that is the motherland the mother's milk the blanket
where we shivered / where we played about /
don't forget the reasons for the exile/
the military dictatorship / the errors
we commited for you / against you /
the land that made us and kneels
at our feet / like dawn outstretched /
and you / my precious heart that watches
at every morning as it fades /
don't you forget to forget to forget it.


09-05-1980

## VIII

We don't queue at the dream factory. We queue in the front of the country. We are living in a dream factory, eating, sleeping, living, they're all dreams, every day we make dreams and we come back for them the next day or dream.

I'm dreaming of the Via del Corso and Jorge is dreaming of the Rue Mouffetard. Dream streets, turned away from us, they'll never know us. We walk down them night and day, we pass them by, we bleed to death on them, we even cry on them, stone dreams that hear other feet.

Our ghostly glare terrifies them. They dream we don't exist, that we don't walk down them.

Barbaric dream street: you have undreamed me entirely.

11-05-1980

# SHASH TREVETT

In June 1956, the Sinhalese nationalist government of Sri Lanka, led by S. W. R. D. Bandaranaike, passed an Act of Parliament stating that the Tamil language would no longer be recognised as one of the national languages of the country. In doing so, the government sought both to impose a Sinhalese doctrinal hegemony over the Tamil people, and to disenfranchise a section of the population uneducated in the Sinhala language. Birth and death certificates, hospital records, job applications could no longer be filled in by the Tamil population, and this led to protests on Galle Face Green in the heart of Colombo. The law was repealed a few years later.

I have used both English and Tamil when writing about this case of glottophagy (or 'linguicide'). It seems inconceivable when writing about the threatened loss of my mother tongue, not to draw on the beauty of its cadences (in Tamil as well as in translation) within my poem. There are a couple of things to note. In the lines 'And when we dreamed | our dreams erupted | in அs and இs and உs', the அ, இ, உ (Aaa, Eee, Ooo) are the first three letters of the Tamil alphabet. Later I refer to the *Tolkkaapiyam*. This is the earliest written Tamil grammar, believed to have originated, in written form from oral sources, sometime between fifth and tenth centuries BC. This text is a fundamental cornerstone of Tamil Literature.

I left Sri Lanka in the late 1980s after the brutal intervention of the Indian Peace Keeping Force. Under them, I learnt to fear the Tamil language itself. My family, and those around me, stopped speaking Tamil on the streets, switching to English, as a way of protecting ourselves from the accusation of being Tamil Tigers. My mother, when negotiating with the Indian soldiers for food or safe passage, or when pleading with them as they lined us up to be shot, spoke to them in Hindi. This was the language of the conqueror, the language of solidarity with the oppressor, the language of

submission. Tamil on the other hand was the feared marker of
aggression, of difference, signifying a strength which the Indian
soldiers feared, and which they caused us to fear in turn. When I
arrived in the UK as a deeply traumatised refugee, I refused to speak
in Tamil. And even now, 30 years later, I cannot speak it. I stutter,
stammer and the words get stuck in my throat. Ironically, in my
case, the wishes of the post-independence Sri Lankan government
have been realised. I can think in Tamil, and write in it, but my
mouth cannot utter the Tamil words that my heart and mind
formulate. I commit linguicide every day that I choose not to speak
Tamil to my children. I believe in a polyglot future, but I yearn to
sing the lullabies of my Tamil past.

## Glottophagy

Tamil words that lilt
soothing as a lullaby on a mother's breath.
Their *isaioli*, their music
nourishing our *uyir*,                                    (life)
marked on a stave
imagined a few millennia ago.
In whispers of promises they show themselves
as *paadal*                                              (songs)
and *kathai*                                             (stories)
and *kavithai*:                                          (poetry)
the Goddess's gifts from her river throne.
Our generations were formed by their fluid *naatiyam*     (dance)
our voices modulated by their scripted *sangheetham*.    (hymns)
And when we dreamed,
our dreams erupted

in அs and இs and உs:
building blocks of a nation
now without a homeland,
a people now without a place.

And when in '56
with the Sinhala Only Act
they tried to silence your *innisai* –
the sweetness of your melody –
gag your *uyiroli*                                                    (vowels)
and eradicate your *meiyelluthal*,                      (consonants)
we took to the streets –
carrying your truth as our arms.
Warriors of the *Tolkkaapiyam*
on Galle Face Green,
paying with our blood for your right to be.
*Oru naadillaathe aatkal*
a people without a country,
in exile,
bearing the music of your beauty, still.

# ESSAYS & REVIEWS

## *Those Destined to Bear Witness*

*Lost Evenings, Lost Lives*, translated and edited by Lakshmi Holmström and Sascha Ebeling, Arc Publications, 2015

*Lost Evenings, Lost Lives*, is a bilingual anthology of Tamil poetry. The poems, arranged in broadly chronological order, trace the events of the civil war in Sri Lanka, as witnessed and absorbed by the Tamil poets in question. Beginning in 1977 and ending in 2015, the 32 anthologised poets have been elegantly and sensitively translated, capturing in English the lyrical sparsity of the Tamil originals, bringing to a new audience the beauty of a language which has poetry at its core. From the first to the last, the poems presented are a map guiding the reader through the suffering of the Tamil people over the last thirty-five years; signposts to the bloody history of the people in the North and East of Sri Lanka.

The detached, unobtrusive editorial stance makes this volume of poetry a pleasure to read. Tamil is a hard language to translate into English. As Lakshmi Holmström has written elsewhere, the syntax works very differently in Tamil and English sentences. In Tamil, the principal verb appears at the end of the sentence leading to inversions and the problems associated with them during translation. Yet the poems presented here read effortlessly. At a quick glance the topography of source and object appear to correspond to each other. A closer examination reveals the skills of both translators: with precision of intent and thought, each difficult Tamil idiom or cadence has been found its English partner. There are no fillers or additions. The poets' own words are presented to the English reader with the integrity and strength of their Tamil originals. What appears in this anthology are poignant and beautiful Tamil poems, translated sympathetically into cleverly crafted and lyrical English counterparts.

Many poems in this volume are worthy of mention and it is hard to single out any for particular attention. Needless to say, the following poems have been picked as they serve the purposes of this review. The volume opens with the elegant 'Last Evening, This Morning' by M. A. Nuhman, from whose final couplet the title of the anthology is taken. He describes lazy days in Jaffna before the war, browsing among bookshops, smoking and chatting by tea stalls, watching busy people living their lives in unrestricted freedom. The land was theirs, the streets, the days, their lives were theirs. That was yesterday. But in the second part of the poem, the today, there is a dramatic, apocalyptic shift. Now the streets are owned by 'khaki-clad men' and

> bullets rain
> piercing bodies
> drinking up lives.

The market place is a smouldering ruin, shops lie desecrated, burning tyres mark the burning of bodies and dreams. The poem was written in 1977 in response to the anti-Tamil riots following the presidential elections of that year. The bewilderment of the poem mirrors that felt by the Tamil people themselves, as they woke to a new reality, bereft of days and nights they could call their own.

The anthology then moves through the years, with poems marking the burning of the Jaffna Public Library (M. A. Nuhman 'Buddha Lay Dead') and the corresponding loss of priceless classical Tamil writings, through to the violence of 1983. Cheran's well-known poem 'I Could Forget All This' speaks graphically and brutally about the events of Black July, when a state-sponsored mob ravaged the streets of Colombo, armed with census forms which enabled them to target Tamil homes and business. An estimated 3,000 Tamil people lost their lives, and a further 150,000 were rendered homeless. Cheran writes of 'thigh bones protruding', a face 'empty of its eye | a socket caked in blood'. The plaintive image of

> A Sinhala woman, pregnant,
> bearing, unbearably,
> a cradle from a burning house

has been poignantly translated by Lakshmi Holmström. Not only does the reader mourn the death of the original occupant of that cradle, but Cheran mourns too the death of a future, of the generations that were lost in those dark days of 1983. From there the anthology moves through the brutal intervention by the Indian Peace Keeping Force, to Mullaivaikkal in 2009, where more than 40,000 Tamil civilians were massacred in the No Fire Zone. The tragedy of the war in Sri Lanka, the mindset that enabled a government to turn its guns on its own people, the peace that is still being denied Tamil people on that island, is best summed up by Dushyanthan in 'They Do Not Know':

> They do not know
> that you and I are human.
>
> All they know is
> that you and I
> are not human.

A wide variety of poets are featured in this volume, encompassing many positions and viewpoints. There are poems by LTTE combatants with their rhetoric of martyrdom and the glorification of the heroic dead, which sit alongside poems more condemnatory of the violence of the liberation struggle. Poems by Muslim Tamils, who suffered greatly under the hands of the LTTE in 1990, make a welcome inclusion. There are various poems about exile and dislocation, about identity and a loss of community, poems about hope for a future peace. What makes this anthology all the more laudable is that many of the poets featured still live and work in the North and East of Sri Lanka. Through these translations we are able to hear their voices and see their words reaching out through time and space, bringing with it a special kind of responsibility to the reader.

Women poets feature strongly in this anthology. Of the 32 poets present, 14 are women. Rape and the consequences of it are a common thread between the women, but they also write eloquently about hope and of loss. S. Sivaramani in her 'Oppressed By Nights Of War' writes starkly about the loss of innocence amongst the children born amidst gunfire and destruction.

> Across the pathways
> of their bright
> fledgling-mornings
> faceless and bloodied
> corpses are flung; [...]
> And our little ones
> are children no longer.

Sivaramani, who was an outspoken critic of the Tamil Tigers, burned her poems before committing suicide in 1991. She was 24 years old and her death went largely unnoticed. She did not die a martyr's death by biting a cyanide capsule or by blowing herself up for the cause. Kutti Revathi writes of such a death in her poem 'Suicide Soldier', sympathetically portraying the effects of patriarchy on female fighters:

> The leader's command
> made your heart a bomb
> caught, swinging, in the web
> held between his two hands.

But as the Black Tiger explodes her body, the reader's sympathy is directed away from her to the 'thirty people... sacrificed' that day as she stepped:

> into the last quarter-minute in the map
> of each person's life there.

Mothers weep as they search for their missing daughters (Malathi Maithri 'Lost Tiger'), wives contemplate lives put on hold (Urvasi 'Do You Understand?'), women mourn the loss of love as the war takes it toll (Faheema Jahan 'The Sea's Waters'). These poems stand as evidence of the flourishing of writing by women during the civil war, a response to the brutalisation of the world around them.

*Lost Evenings, Lost Lives* not only brings to a wider audience excellent Tamil poetry, it also performs an important political service. During the long years of the civil war, the government of Sri Lanka maintained a news blackout on events occurring in the North and East. The world was kept in ignorance of the atrocities being committed there, by both sides of the conflict. But during these dark times, Tamil poets were witnessing and writing about events unfolding around them. Holmström and Ebeling by translating these poems written under duress, state clearly that Tamil lives do matter and Tamil words will speak. As P. Ahilan writes in his poem '2005':

> together with those destined to bear witness
> there I sat.

Lakshmi Holmström and Sascha Ebeling have not merely sat and watched. They have brought to light writings that need to be read, disseminated, discussed and appreciated, so that the world can never again say, we did not know.

*Shash Trevett*

# A Sensitive Earthquake Zone

Yu Xiang, *I Can Almost See the Clouds of Dust*, translated by Fiona Sze-Lorrain, Zephyr Press and The Chinese University Press, 2013

Lan Lan, *Canyon in the Body*, translated by Fiona Sze-Lorrain, Zephyr Press and The Chinese University Press, 2014

It's a miraculous thing, the give-and-take of translations across time and space. Mallarmé's fascination with Poe's 'The Raven' comes to mind, but also how, having translated it, Mallarmé then borrowed the poem's mournful rhyme sounds ('lore... door... more') for his 'Sonnet in –yx' ('amphore...sonore...'); and how English poets go on struggling to carry Mallarmé's highly wrought verse across linguistic borders. Translators will say they undertake translations, in part, to enrich the linguistic and formal possibilities of the target language – but almost always, especially when the translator is also a poet, the enrichment begins at home.

The single most memorable instance of this expansion of possibilities in the recent past must be the discovery of classical (principally T'ang) Chinese poetry early in the twentieth century. The poems in Ezra Pound's 1915 collection, *Cathay*, captured the imagination of English-language readers and poets, and have influenced English poetic writing from the Imagists, including Pound himself ('Faces in a Metro') and William Carlos Williams, to the work of a contemporary Chinese-American poet like Arthur Sze, as a few lines from 'Chrysalis,' in Sze's 2009 collection *The Gingko Light* will show:

> The wisteria along the porch never blooms;
> a praying mantis on the wood floor sips water
>
> from a dog bowl. Laughter from upstairs echoes...

Syntactical parallelism and juxtaposition of images, whose links to one another must be teased out, shape the page: Sze has said his poems are influenced 'by the motion of classical Chinese poetry (in the way that a five or seven character line unfolds)... translating classical Chinese poetry was an essential stage in the development of my own poetry.'

That China's influence on English language poetry is a two-way street is one thing Fiona Sze-Lorrain's sound-conscious (Sze-Lorrain, a Singaporian who lives in France, is a musician as well as a poet) translations of two contemporary Chinese poets, Yu Xiang and Lan Lan, born in 1970 and 1967 respectively, demonstrates. For anyone used to the shape of T'ang poetry, it is striking to see the Chinese characters here fall down the left page, not in blocks, but in varying-length lines like English free verse. Grammatical parallelism is used and images can be simply juxtaposed as in classical Chinese poetry, but logical connectives and markers of time and place may complicate the syntax. Nature is present as we might expect, but so are cities and contemporary life with its pleasures, its technology and sciences, and its violence: the ineffable – the '"beyond words" towards which Chinese poetry has always tended' (François Cheng, *Chinese Poetic Writing*) is de-emphasized. And whereas the suppression of personal pronouns in classical Chinese poems gives them an air of impersonality, in these two books, both by women, whose voices were rarely heard, though often impersonated in the classical poem, human dramas occupy the foreground, and the women shed their traditionally submissive, muse-like role, and become subjects in their own right.

Yu Xiang's *I Can Almost See the Clouds of Dust* contains ten groups of poems (regrettably it is not clear, in either book, whether there is a chronology in the poems' ordering) opening with 'My House':

I have a door, a reminder:
*Be careful!*
You might lose your way.
This is my house, a long narrow
hallway, a table with a view.
[...]
I have a chair. Sometimes
it disappears.

The language is plain, the syntax simple as a primer, the tone
conversational. Several poems have irony-tinged socio-political
comment ('classroom buildings under construction | as cost-effective
as possible, gaudy and pompous | even in a sensitive earthquake
zone'), but most evoke the quotidian: love affairs, self-doubt,
dysfunctional families, domestic activities ('I squat on the balcony
picking Chinese leeks'). Objects can seem surrealistically mysterious
or menacing (the disappearing chair, above). The poems are often
held together with repetition, as in 'To the One Who Writes Poetry
Tonight,' a 10-page poem of precise detail, *bribes* of narration and
something like prayer, punctuated with thoughts and feelings.

In Lan Lan's *Canyon in the Body* the five groups of poems depict
a range of personal experience ('I am the book I once read | the wall
I leaned on...| am a mother's breast and a baby's mouth'). If some
of the tonal and syntactical ruptures in the earlier sections of her
book are jagged ('What is more is silence. | A secret magnetic needle
among wild geese. || Many smiles emerge from the crowd... .'), leaps
in the volume's later poems are easier to follow. Here, for instance, is
'Parasitic Bacteria':

Abandoned mines, pits accumulated with water.
Stove fire in your chest is long out.

Could it have lived in blazing times
when we still didn't know the cold?

I unbutton my blouse, let the sun dry
the damp moldy heaps of firewood –

Meant for two hands' fiery flames, it is now
growing fungi absurdly.

Note the sure-footedness in the choice of sensuous detail, in the
modulation of sounds ('cold... blouse... firewood... flames... fungi')
and in the poem's suggestive, metonymic shifts from cold to heat
to mould. Why these images and not others? Some of the meaning-
making here is up to the reader. Still, the lines give the feeling of
saying more than first meets the eye.

To the Western reader Lan Lan's and Yu Xiang's poems will
not seem particularly foreign: absent some of the props ('steamed
buns...rice fields') most could be mistaken for English-language
poems. This is partly due to English-language poetry's adoption
of some Chinese poetic techniques. But, as Gao Xingjian, author
of the Nobel Prize-winning novel, *Soul Mountain*, and others have
written, European languages and culture have also influenced the
Chinese vernacular over the past century, moving it towards a more
colloquial and syntactically complex language. Xi Jiang and Lan
Lan know their classics but also clearly their contemporaries and
antecedents in other parts of the world. These two books will enrich
the growing body of contemporary Chinese poetry in translation;
they will also expand the ways in which English readers and writers
understand the Chinese poem.

*Beverley Bie Brahic*

# The Artist and the Poet

Isao Miura and Chris Beckett, *Sketches from the Poem Road, after Matsuo Bashō's The Narrow Road to the Deep North*, Hagi Press, 2015

This is a book brimming with translation, including but not restricted to the linguistic, a work inspired by the notion of continuous change and transformation. The journey starts when Isao Miura, a Japanese artist, through his sketches follows in the footsteps of Matsuo Bashō.

Bashō, the great seventeenth-century Japanese poet and Zen Buddhist, wrote about his precarious physical and spiritual journey through the landscape of his country, which included visits in honour of places associated with other artists. He cast away his possessions and his account is of four journeys, the longest of which 'the long road' lasted two and a half years and took him up to the north of the country, an area familiar to Miura but at that time an unexplored and mysterious territory. *The Narrow Road to the Deep North and other Travel Sketches*, is written in *haibun*, a combination of prose and poetry. This form and in particular the *haiku* poems, so perfect for capturing the fleeting moment of beauty and meaning in a landscape, also sets the tone of the book *Sketches from the Poem Road*.

The sketches are unfinished, preparatory, open to the world, and the book becomes itself with the contribution of poet and translator, Chris Beckett, whose name will be familiar to MPT readers for his collaborations with Ethiopian poets and his translations from Amharic. He initially encouraged Miura in his creations and then started to write in delicate response to Bashō, Miura at work, and to the sketches, his words scattered like touches of a paintbrush across the page.

The book is slightly larger than A4 and is designed as a sketchbook, although with high quality paper and print. Each page contains a charcoal sketch, or a group of words in Western cursive script or occasionally in a brush-stroked Japanese calligraphic character. Translations of Bashō and original work are differentiated by colour, with the translation in blue. Like the original, the form of the writing is *haibun* and it contains poems, exposition, description, as well as translation of Bashō's lines by Beckett and Miura together. The visual impact of the book is significant. The writing has minimum punctuation, words are broken up by spaces and blend seamlessly with the calligraphic images and sketches.

In the Poetry Society exhibition in London that accompanied the book launch, a page stretched horizontally along the left wall representing the road, like a river, painted in a black wash over torn strips of paper. The road also fills the first facing pages of the book and is followed by sketches in pencil and charcoal of a little man walking, dwarfed by the landscape, figures communing in a group, one meditating, a man breaking out of a rock shaped like a teardrop, head high, determined, and myths of monsters and goddesses introduced in Bashō's *haibun* re-surface on these pages.

The sketches were eventually to become the basis for two sculptures, plaster and bronze pieces, displayed at the end of the exhibition, the end of the road. Miura's illustrations look back to his past and Bashō, but they also represent his artistic journey into the future. During the making of this book, he took up a fellowship in the Chelsea College of Art Foundry and for the first time worked in the three-dimensional forms of plaster and bronze, using the lost wax method of bronze casting. And the sculptures have also continued to change in the Foundry, moving through six transitions before the final cleaning, polishing and patination, to emerge in several versions, in green or silver or gold, each surface giving the work a different character.

Meanwhile Beckett watches Miura rest his pencil, like Bashō his pen, and rests his own pen in order to watch, just as Bashō halted on his journey to observe and write about life around him. Then Beckett, in light, sensual poems, picks up his pen again to describe Bashō's journey, while watching Miura at work. A student/master relationship is suggested, mirroring Bashō and his disciple:

> The teardrop of a fish
> bursts out of its sketched eye
> pear bottomed, weighty with plaster
> fish-festooned on the road to bronze
>
> I photograph you
> turning it slowly on the stand
> studying the little man
> who steps so gently, resolutely out of it
>
> just as this poem studies you
> not photo-flat        but in the amazing
> all-around of your body
> which bursts out of nowhere
>
> every time I look at you

In this lovely poem a number of transitions take place and dimensions are explored. The teardrop of the fish is an image taken from Bashō:

> Spring is leaving too!
> Birds cry        even the wet eyes
> Of fish fill with tears

This becomes a sketch by Miura of the little man walking out of a tear-drop shape. The poet observes the artist, considers and photographs him, writes a poem, seeing his 'all-around' body like a moving sculpture, and through the intensity of his watching expresses his own feeling about him.

'Lonely, sad – the landscape of a troubled mind' was how Bashō described the volcano, Mount Chokai in Kisigata Bay in the north of the country towards the end of his journey. A hundred years after Bashō's visit the volcano erupted. When he was in his teens Miura had a job as a guide leading tourists up that mountain and shortly afterwards it erupted for a second time. On each occasion the landscape was transformed. The 'troubled mind' and spiritual darkness are represented towards the end of the book by Miura in black monstrous images of the mountain, but it is followed by the one of the the man stepping out of the teardrop, a hard, rock-like teardrop, a strong final image.

MPT's editorials and content have always suggested that the complex meanings inherent in 'translation' include the idea of making new, a work for now, at the same time as enriching our connection with the past. The sense I was left by this artistic collaboration was of a love poem in which two artists observe, work with one another, hesitate and progress together, their work transforming on its way, together with the great Japanese poet, Matsuo Bashō, their guide from four centuries earlier.

*Caroline Maldonado*

An exhibition of *Sketches from the Poem Road* is being held at the Glass Tank Gallery, Oxford Brookes University from Monday 20 June until Friday 15 July, 2016. The gallery will be open daily from 9am to 5pm, Monday to Friday, and weekends by appointment.

*Further details on the project and Glass Tank Gallery websites:*

- afterBasho.weebly.com
- www.brookes.ac.uk/about-brookes/events/glass-tank/current-and-forthcoming-events

# NOTES ON CONTRIBUTORS

**ANAS AOLO**, an Assyrian poet and dramatist from Baghdede, has published extensively in Iraq's most respected literary journals, such as the literary organ of the Syriac Writers' Union, *Safrutha*. He has received a number of awards for his poetry and plays. He is now living in a makeshift refugee camp in Ankawa, Iraq.

**RACHEL TZVIA BACK** is a poet and translator. Her translations of poems by Tuvia Ruebner in the 2014 bilingual collection *In the Illuminated Dark: Selected Poems of Tuvia Ruebner*, was shortlisted for the National Translation Award in Poetry and was a National Jewish Book Award Finalist.

**CHRIS BECKETT** grew up in Ethiopia in the 1960s. His translation of poems by Bewketu Seyoum, *In Search of Fat*, was published by Flipped Eye in 2012 and his second collection of poems, *Ethiopia Boy*, came out from Carcanet/Oxford Poets in 2013.

**VIKTOR BERBERI** is Assistant Professor of Italian at the University of Minnesota, Morris. He has published English versions of contemporary Italian and Albanian poets and is currently working on a translation of the *Selected Poems of Gëzim Hajdari*, along with a critical survey of Albanian self-representation in Italian literature.

**MANASH 'FIRAQ' BHATTACHARJEE** is a poet, writer, translator and political science scholar. His poems have appeared in *The London Magazine*, *New Welsh Review*, *The Fortnightly Review*, *Elohi Gadugi Journal*, *Mudlark*, *Metamorphoses*, *The Postcolonialist*, *The Missing Slate*. His first collection of poetry, *Ghalib's Tomb and Other Poems* (2013), was published by *The London Magazine*.

**BEVERLEY BIE BRAHIC**'s new collection, *Hunting the Boar* (CB editions) is a Poetry Book Society Recommendation. *White Sheets* (CB Editions, 2012), was a Forward Prize finalist; and her translation of *Apollinaire The Little Auto* won the Scott Moncrieff Prize. Her most recent translation is Yves Bonnefoy's *The Anchor's Long Chain* (Seagull).

**CARMEN BUGAN** is the author of *Crossing the Carpathians; Burying the Typewriter: Childhood Under the Eye of the Secret Police; Seamus Heaney and East European Poetry in Translation: Poetics of Exile* and *The House of Straw*. Her latest collection of poems, *Releasing the Porcelain Birds*, is published this month.

**MADELEINE CAMPBELL** is a writer, researcher and translator. Her translations of Maghrebi poets have appeared in the *University of California Book of North African Literature* (2012) and *Lighthouse* (2015).

**PIERLUIGI CAPPELLO** was born in 1967 in Gemona del Friuli. He has published seven collections of poetry. Among his awards are the Montale Europa prize (2004), the Bagutta Opera Prima prize (2007), and the prestigious Viareggio-Rèpaci prize (2010) for his collection *Mandate a dire all'imperatore* (Crocetti Editore). In 2013, Rizzoli published his selected poems in the volume *Azzurro elementare*.

**JULIA CASTERTON** (1952–2007), poet and teacher, taught creative writing at London's City Lit. In 2004, her first full-length collection of poems, *The Doves of Finisterre* (Rialto), won the Jerwood Aldeburgh First Collection prize.

**BHASKAR CHAKRABORTY** (1945–2005) is a modern Bengali poet and writer. He was born in Baranagar, in the northern part of Calcutta. A teacher by profession, he published many collections of poetry. His debut *When Will It be Winter, Suparna*, in 1971, received immediate acclaim. His prose work includes a collection of his diary and personal journals, published posthumously in 2013. He died of lung cancer in 2005.

**AMARJIT CHANDAN** has published six collections of poetry, and five books of essays in Punjabi. Collections of his poems in English versions include *Being Here* (1995, 1999, 2005), *Sonata for Four Hands* prefaced by John Berger (Arc, 2010), *The Parrot, The Horse & The Man* (Arc, due in 2016)

**DAVID COLMER** is an Australian writer and translator and the winner of several translation prizes. He focuses on Dutch and Flemish literature, but occasionally translates German and, very occasionally, Indonesian – the latter with a lot of help from his friends.

**MOLLY CRABAPPLE** is an artist, journalist, and author of the memoir *Drawing Blood*. Called 'An emblem of the way art can break out of the gilded gallery' by the *New Republic*, she has drawn in and reported from Guantanamo Bay, Abu Dhabi's migrant labour camps, and in Syria, Lebanon, Gaza, the West Bank, and Iraqi Kurdistan.

**CHRISTINE DE LUCA**, who writes in both English and Shetlandic, is a native Shetlander who lives in Edinburgh. She was appointed Edinburgh's Makar (poet laureate) in 2014. Her latest collection, *Dat Trickster Sun* (Mariscat 2014) was shortlisted for the Michael Marks Poetry Pamphlet Prize.

**NED DENNY** was born in London in 1975. His poems have appeared in *PN Review, Poetry Review, The White Review* and the *TLS*.

**MOHAMMED DIB** (1920–2003) was born in Tlemcen. He is a key founder of Francophone Algerian literature with over twenty novels, several collections of short stories and nine poetry collections.

**TENZIN DICKIE**'s poetry and essays have appeared in *Indian Literature, Seminar Magazine, Apogee Journal, Tibetan Review, Cultural Anthropology* and the anthologies *Voices in Exile* and *The Yellow Nib: Modern English Poetry by Indians*. Her translations have appeared in *The Washington Post* online and *Words Without Borders*. She was a 2014 fellow of the American Literary Translators' Association.

**DON MEE CHOI** is the author of *Hardly War* (Wave Books, April 2016), *The Morning News Is Exciting* (Action Books, 2010), and translator of contemporary Korean women poets.

**EMMA GEE** is a lecturer in Classics at St Andrews. She has published academic books on Ovid, and on Aratus' 'Phaenomena', an astronomical poem of the third century CE, and its Latin translations.

**JUAN GELMAN**'s (1930–2014) first poetry collection was published in 1956. Following the Argentine Coup in 1976, Gelman was forced into exile in Europe, his son, daughter and pregnant daughter-in-law were 'disappeared' during the dictatorship. In 2007, he received the Cervantes Prize, the Spanish language literature prize for lifetime achievement.

**GEMORAW** was an Ethiopian poet, academic, linguist and democracy campaigner born in Addis Ababa in 1935. He was forced to flee in the mid 1970s to China, then Norway and Sweden. He died in Sweden in November, 2014.

**ELIZABETH T. GRAY, JR.** is a poet, translator, and corporate consultant. *SERIES | INDIA*, a collection of original poems, was published by Four Way Books in 2015. Her translations from classical and contemporary Persian include *The Green Sea of Heaven: Fifty Ghazals from the Diwan-i Hafiz-i Shirazi* (1995) and *Iran: Poems of Dissent* (2013). www.elizabethtgrayjr.com.

**OLAV GRINDE** recently published *Luminous Spaces: Olav H. Hauge: Selected Poems & Journals* (White Pine Press, Buffalo, 2016), and previously *Night Open: Selected Poems of Rolf Jacobsen* (White Pine Press, 1993).

**BASUKI GUNAWAN** was an Indonesian sociologist who lived and worked in the Netherlands and wrote in Indonesian, Dutch and English. Besides several academic books, he published poetry, short stories and a novella. He also translated Indonesian poetry into Dutch, in collaboration with his wife Liselotte Gunawan-Grote.

**BAYDAA HADAYA**, an Assyrian poet from Baghdede, Nineveh Plains (now under ISIS control), writes both in Assyrian and Arabic and is a member of Baghdede Literary Forum. She has performed and published her poetry in Iraq's most respected literary festivals and journals. After a long displacement, Hadaya has now moved to the USA.

**GËZIM HAJDARI** was born in Lushnje, Albania in 1957 and fled his homeland for Italy in 1992. He has received numerous awards for his poetry and is considered a leading voice among migrant poets writing in Italian. He publishes his poetry in rigorously dual-language collections, as he writes in both Albanian and Italian and resists the notion of either version as a translation of an original.

**GOLAN HAJI** is a Syrian Kurdish poet and translator who currently lives in France. His most recent poetry collection *Autumn Here is Magical and Vast* was published in a bilingual Arabic/Italian edition by Il Sirente, Rome, 2013. His latest translation is Alberto Manguel's *A Reader on Reading*, Dar Al- Saqi, Beirut, 2016.

**BARZAN ABDUL GHANI JARJIS** is an Assyrian poet and novelist from Baghdede, Nineveh Plains and a member of the Syriac Writers' Union and the Al-Hadbaa Forum for Folk Poetry in Mosul. Like many other writers from Baghdede, he too is living in a makeshift refugee camp in Ankawa, Iraq.

**LOUISE LABÉ** (c.1522–66) published her *Works* (sonnets, elegies and a prose dialogue) in 1555. They met with both notoriety and success.

**NINEB LAMASSU** writes his poetry in the Modern Assyrian language and his poetry has been translated into English, Spanish, Swedish, Arabic, Turkish, Kurdish and Farsi. His recently published collection *Stolen Title* refers to the centennial of the Assyrian, Armenian and Pontus-Greek genocide of 1915 and ISIS crimes in Syria and Iraq.

**CAROLINE MALDONADO** is a poet and translator. Recent publications include her pamphlet of poems *What they say in Avenale* (Indigo Dreams Publishing 2014) and *Your call keeps us awake*, (Smokestack 2013), poems by Rocco Scotellaro co-translated with Allen Prowle from Italian. She lives in London and Italy.

**CAITLÍN MAUDE** (1941–1982) was an Irish poet, playwright, actress and traditional singer. A volume of her collected poems was published posthumously by Coiscéim.

**OLIVIA MCCANNON**'s translations include Balzac's *Old Man Goriot*. Her poetry collection *Exactly My Own Length* won the Fenton Aldeburgh First Collection Prize.

**ANDRÉ NAFFIS-SAHELY** translates fiction and poetry from the French and the Italian. His debut collection of poetry *The Promised Land* will be published by Penguin in 2017.

**MAJID NAFICY** fled Iran in 1983, a year and a half after the execution of his wife Ezzat in Tehran. Since 1984 Majid has lived in West Los Angeles. Naficy's poetry has been widely anthologized, and he has published two collections of poetry in English, *Muddy Shoes* (Beyond Baroque, Books, 1999) and *Father and Son* (Red Hen Press, 2003).

**DOIREANN NÍ GHRÍOFA** is a bilingual poet, awarded the Ireland Chair of Poetry Bursary by Paula Meehan. Her first collection of poems in English is *Clasp*.

**ABDALLA NURI** writes in both Assyrian and Arabic. He has two published collections and his poetry has been published in a number of Middle Eastern literary journals. He is also a member of the Syriac Writers' Union and a member of the Iraqi Writers' Union. Nuri is from Baghdede on the Nineveh Plains but is currently living in a makeshift refugee camp in Ankawa, Iraq.

**JAMIE OSBORN** founded Cambridge Student PEN to support human rights for writers and through writing both locally and internationally. Updates on Cambridge Student PEN's work are posted at: www.facebook.com/officialcambridgeunipen

**NASRIN PARVAZ** became a civil rights activist when the Islamic regime took power in Iran. She was arrested, tortured and sentenced to death in 1982. She fled to England after her release, where she claimed asylum in 1993. She was granted refugee status a year later, and has since lived in London. Nasrin's prison memoir was published in Farsi in 2002 and was published in Italian in 2006 by Effedue Edizioni.

**KEITH PAYNE** is the Ireland Chair of Poetry Bursary Award winner for 2015-2016. His debut collection, *Broken Hill*, (Lapwing Publications, 2015), will be followed by *Six Galician Poets*, (Arc Publications, 2016). Keith lives in Vigo, Galicia with the musician Su Garrido Pombo.

**AMIR POLIS IBRAHIM** is an Assyrian poet and novelist from Baretle, Nineveh Plains (now under ISIS control). He writes both in Assyrian and Arabic. He is a member of the Syriac and Iraqi Writers' Union. He currently lives in a makeshift refugee camp in Ankawa, Iraq.

**CLARE POLLARD**'s most recent collection *Changeling* was a Poetry Book Society Recommendation. Her latest book, a new version of *Ovid's Heroines*, is currently touring as a one-woman show with Jaybird Live Literature. Her website is www.clarepollard.com

**TODD PORTNOWITZ**'s poems, Italian translations, and essays have appeared in *PN Review, Virginia Quarterly Review, Southwest Review, Poesia, Poetry Salzburg Review, AGNI* and elsewhere. He is co-founder and co-editor of the Italian poetry blog, *Formavera*, and a poetry editor with the Sheep Meadow Press.

**CAROLINE PRICE** is a musician and writer living in Kent. She has published short stories and three collections of poetry, most recently *Wishbone* (Shoestring Press 2008), and has translated poetry and prose for the 44th and 45th International Poetry Festivals in Rotterdam (2013 and 2014).

**YOUSIF M. QASMIYEH** is Lector in Arabic at the Oxford University Language Centre. His poetry and translations have appeared in *Critical Quarterly, Modern Poetry in Translation*, and *GeoHumanities*.

**ARNE RUSTE**'s first collection, *Askeladd* (Ash Lad), was published in 1973. He has published ten poetry collections, culminating in 2012 in a Collected, *Kretsløp* (Flow) 2012, which includes newer 'Occasional Poems', 2002-2012. He has translated several Sufi poets as well as Ted Hughes and the war poems of Wilfred Owen (2014); and rhymes for children by Roald Dahl and Julia Donaldson.

**RIBKA SIBHATU** (1962–) was born in Eritrea and writes in Tigrinya and Italian. She was unjustly imprisoned for a year in 1979 and on her release she fled to Ethiopia. She now lives in Italy and combines writing and activism on behalf of migrants.

**ALEMU TEBEJE** is an Ethiopian journalist, poet and web-campaigner based in London. His poems have been published in the anthologies *Forever Spoken* and *No Serenity Here*, featuring 26 poets from 12 African countries. His website is: www.debteraw.com

**HABIB TENGOUR** is an Algerian writer, poet and anthropologist. Born in Mostaganem in 1947, he and his family moved to France while he was still a child and he travels between and lectures in both countries. He is considered a major voice among contemporary North African Francophone writers. A selection of his work translated into English by Pierre Joris, *Exile is my Trade*, was published in 2012 by Black Widow Press.

**MAYA TEVET DAYAN** (1975–) is an Israeli poet and writer currently residing in Canada. Her poems have been translated into English and Russian and have appeared in books and various other venues. She holds a PhD in Sanskrit Poetry and is currently a visiting scholar at the University of British Columbia.

**SHASH TREVETT** is a Tamil from Sri Lanka, who came to the UK to escape from the civil war. She has been published in MPT and *Interpreters House*. She read at the First World War commemoration events in Yorkshire, and at the 2015 York Literature Festival. She has been recorded by the British Library sound archive for their 'Between Two Worlds: Poetry & Translation Project'.

**HAMA TUMA** is an important Ethiopian political activist, poet and writer of satirical articles and short stories. His first collection of stories, *The Case of the Socialist Witch Doctor and Other Stories*, was published by Heinemann London in 1993. He lives in Paris. His website is www.hamatuma.com

**WANG WEI WANG WEI** (699–761), a contemporary of the better known Li Po and Tu Fu, was in his lifetime as celebrated for his paintings as for his poetry. He had a successful career as a court official, yet after the deaths of his wife and mother spent increasing periods in the solitude of his Wang (literally 'wheel rim') River estate.

**STEPHEN WATTS** is a poet, translator and long-time contributor to MPT. His collection *Republic of Dogs / Republic of Birds* was published in 2016 by Test Centre.